MW01164867

Seeds of Lotus: Cambodian and Vietnamese Voices in America

©2006 Peggy Rambach
The Paper Journey Press
an Imprint of Sojourner Publishing, Inc.
Wake Forest, NC USA

All rights reserved. Printed in the United States of America

No part of this book maybe reproduced or transmitted in any form
or by any means, electronic or mechanical, including photocopying,
recording, or by any information and storage and retrieval system,
without written permission from the publisher, editor, or pertinent
author.

Views expressed within these pages are those of the authors and do
not represent the views of Sojourner Publishing, Inc. or its imprints.
Every effort was made to verify spelling of translated Vietnamese and
Cambodian towns, villages and their inhabitants.

The Paper Journey Press: www.thepaperjourney.com
First trade paperback edition
Manufactured in the United States of America

Asian Center of Merrimack Valley, Inc.
1 Ballard Way
Lawrence, MA 01843
978-683-7316
asiancentermv.org

Cover Painting by Rosalvo Leomeu Vidal
Cover design by Mark Nedostup
Interior Design by Dan Russell
Interior Photos by Cheryl Senter
Library of Congress Control Number: 2006932257
International Standard Book Number (ISBN) 0977315665

Seeds of Lotus

✼

Cambodian and Vietnamese
Voices in America

EDITED BY PEGGY RAMBACH

The Paper Journey Press
Wake Forest, NC

Seeds of Lotus: Cambodian and Vietnamese Voices in America

Acknowledgments

I wish to thank Sister Elana Killilea, former director of the Asian Center of Merrimack Valley Inc., for envisioning all three writing workshops that produced this book. She sought to provide the Cambodian and Vietnamese communities of the Merrimack Valley in Massachusetts a way to be visible and to be heard while encouraging their sense of community and self-worth. I also thank Sister Elana for our collaboration and her tireless pursuit of funding. Therefore she and I and the Asian Center wish to acknowledge the generosity of our funders: The Sisters of Charity, the Lawrence Cultural Council and the Massachusetts Cultural Council.

This book would not exist if many had not generously offered their skills and their time. Thank you to Nikki Toeur, Hue Nguyen, and Sister Le-Hang Le who translated the stories as they were being told and gave me advice and support throughout our workshops. And I am also thankful for the assistance of Elaine McKinnon, Bruce Sharp, Kevin McDermott, The Pike School 2003 ninth grade class, The City of Lawrence, Massachusett's Senior Center, Jeanette Recina, Chong Nguyen of the Joiner Center at the University of Massachusetts Boston, Catherine Hinsdale and George Whisstock of Bmarkweb, and Mark Nedostup, Cheryl Senter, Rosalvo Leomeu Vidal and Wanda Wade Mukherjee.

Finally, I am deeply grateful to the contributors who told us their stories with humor, grace and courage.

Peggy Rambach

i

Seeds of Lotus: Cambodian and Vietnamese Voices in America

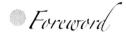# Foreword

The Vietnam War destabilized the entire region of Southeast Asia forcing refugees from Vietnam, Cambodia and Laos to pass through Thailand, Singapore, Malaysia, Indonesia and the Philippines, their final destinations unknown and their futures uncertain.

Many spent years in camps, hoping to begin a new life, every aspect of which would be foreign to them – the language, food, weather, clothing, and social customs. By the mid-1980's, a significant number of Southeast Asians had settled in and around Lawrence, a city in the northeastern corner of Massachusetts.

Sister Helen O'Leary and Sister Barbara Sullivan of the Sisters of Charity, observed the surge in the city's population of Asians, recognized their need for transitional assistance, and in 1987 founded the Seton Asian Center.

Nearly twenty years later, the Seton Asian Center has moved to larger quarters, is now called the Asian Center of Merrimack Valley Inc. and continues to welcome Asian immigrants with the programs and support that helps them begin their lives successfully in America.

Seeds of Lotus: Cambodian and Vietnamese Voices in America

Table of Contents

Under the Sugar Palm Trees

Means of Escape

● *A Name Like Me*

Under the
Sugar Palm Trees

Seeds of Lotus: Cambodian and Vietnamese Voices in America

To the Children

Seeds of Lotus: Cambodian and Vietnamese Voices in America

Introduction

We gathered around a long table for two hours, twice a week, for six weeks in a bright first-floor room at the Lawrence Senior Center. Not everyone there was a Senior. The participants ranged in age from their mid-thirties to late-seventies. Each came with a story to tell or simply a desire to listen.

The translator, Nikki Toeur, sat to my left, and to my right were pair of ninth grade students from the Pike School in Andover, Massachusetts, who took turns attending the sessions to help me scribe. They wrote these impressions of the experience:

Sometimes it is hard to grasp how powerful people are to fight through things like this and how easy we have it…We live and think in our own little world and there's a much larger community than what we think of…All my life, I've heard about wars and issues throughout the world, but had never heard stories from people who had experienced them first-hand.

I asked questions. When Sopheap Yin said she walked from Phnom Penh to the border of Thailand, I asked her how long it took. "A year," she said. When I asked her what she wore on her feet, she said, "Nothing."

I also asked the participants to describe the landscape and found many of them mentioned the sugar palm tree. Its fronds provided shelter and the sugar made from its nectar sealed marriages, and in trade, staved off starvation. It rose, a constant on the Cambodian landscape, no matter what happened beneath it.

For all of us it was a rare privilege to enter that room in a simple brick building on Haverhill Street in Lawrence, Massachusetts, and now it is a privilege to present to a greater audience the stories we heard there.

Seeds of Lotus: Cambodian and Vietnamese Voices in America

Ban Sat

Born 1947

When I was ten years old, my room was filled with white pillows and blankets. We had no beds. Only the higher classes had beds. I remember my blankets were a mix of gray and white, a little bit of everything, and mosquito nets hung from the ceiling. There was nothing to play with. It smelled of roach urine. The roaches lived in the leaves that the hut was made from. The smell is almost like human urine but very bad. The roaches in Cambodia are as big as your thumb. If they spray on you and you don't clean it off, the urine will eat at your skin.

When I walked in that room, I thought about growing up. What was I going to have? I didn't have a mother and my father was in the army and he ran away to Thailand. I lived with my grandmother.

First thing in the morning I cooked and served food to the monks for blessings, rice and fish and pickles. I'd water the plants and afterwards I would go to school. After school I would go to the forest to pick fruit and sell it to buy clothes. This was not being poor because I could go to school and we had a small piece of land to plant.

My marriage was arranged. My husband was a quiet man. I had to speak to him first before he spoke to me. I didn't hate him, but I can't say I really loved him.

One day when I was sixteen years old, an old lady came to my village and asked me if I had a picture of myself. She was going to take it to my husband's village. He was thirty-five and looking for a wife. I gave her the picture and asked if she could give me a picture of him, but he didn't have one. I accepted his proposal anyway, though, because I'd already refused two men. If I refused too many men I'd shame my grandmother. But when people found out I was going to marry him, they said, "Ew! Why are you going to marry that guy! His skin is too dark. He's ugly!" I wanted to run away then, but I didn't because I didn't want to humiliate my grandmother.

The people in my husband's village heard that I was beautiful. When I got there, they all stared at me. After they saw me some joked around and asked him if he'd like to exchange wives, but he would just smile. It didn't bother him. Every time my husband went shopping, though, he didn't want to bring me because people thought I was his daughter or his servant.

For the first week of our marriage, every time he touched me I'd jump. I didn't sleep and wrapped a lot of blankets around me so I could protect myself from him. I had circles under my eyes. I was scared of him and wouldn't even eat with him.

Every time he went away, though, I'd cry and run after him, even when I was pregnant. And when I was pregnant I'd still jump in the water and make bubbles with my skirt and have fun like a child. I wasn't careful. I climbed trees and jumped rope. I only realized slowly that I should start eating better and caring for myself.

When I had my first baby I was in the house beating the husks off the rice. All of a sudden I started having contractions. I worked in the fields every day, so when my relatives didn't see me there, they figured that I was having the baby and came in to find me. My grandmother and aunt were there. I didn't know what it would be like. Every time I had a contraction I pinched my aunt. My labor only lasted a half hour.

My husband stayed outside to make a fire, prepare hot water and wash clothes. We just wrapped cloths around the baby. There were no diapers. People came afterwards and gave us one or two riels. For a first baby there are some gifts.

After having a baby you have to stay in bed for seven days. You have to eat only warm foods. You can't eat or touch anything cold. You also drink an alcoholic drink that's had an herb soaked in it for three or four months. It helps the bad blood come out after the baby is born. Also, after the eighth month, if you drink for seven days a liquor called sra, mixed with the whites of eggs, then the baby will come out quickly and cleanly.

After my first child, I also had twins, two boys, but one son died at three months. The other is now twenty-three years old. With twins you have to go to ten houses to ask for food, money and gifts. If the twins are both boys, you tie them together to be sure they are always best friends. If the twins are a boy and a girl, you marry them as a way to ensure they stay together, that one doesn't die.

When my baby died, I wrapped it in thick material and buried it on a hill where water wouldn't collect. You could pick your own place for burial. Many people are buried near temples and many people are buried on their farms. You can be buried or cremated. My mother wanted to be cremated. But when you're cremated, it's not done inside. You burn the body in a field and you can smell the smoke and it smells like you're cooking something.

Because of the hunger in 1979, my husband died. He died of dysentery. There was no one to support the family. I had four children. I heard you could get free food at the camp in Thailand. So I made one trip and got rice for my children and mother, and then I came home. Then I made a second trip with my brother and my ten-year-old son. My brother was about twenty years old. He was light-skinned and short.

When we reached the border of the camp, we stayed with a friend. Her name was Cheang. She and her husband told me I should leave Cambodia. "You should live at the camp," they said. "There's free food. It's better here."

My brother said, "Yes. Let's make a place to live before we bring the rest of the family here." They were three days and three nights away.

I agreed and said, "Let's go find some small trees to make a hut." I asked Cheang, "Where would I find some bushes to make a hut?"

She said, "There are small trees and bushes by a stream."

We all went: Cheang, me, my brother, my son and Cheang's son. When we crossed the stream we didn't see the sign that had on it a picture of a ghost with an X over it. But I saw a can and a string. I stepped back, but my brother had crossed the stream already. He was two steps in front of me. I said, "Stop. And come back slowly." But when he stepped back the mine exploded.

His intestines were coming out of his body. I carried him on my back. I took him to the Red Cross. We rode a truck to a temple on the border. I had told my son to stay behind, but when I got to the temple, I turned around and my son was there. I said, "How did you get here?" He must have taken a short cut and run the whole way.

At the temple, there was blood all over the place. My brother was screaming and said he wished he had died because he was hurting so much. They put his intestines in a bag to hold them in. The Thai said they would bring him to a hospital and he would survive. Once he was at the hospital they said, "Do you want to see your brother?" and I said, yes.

That's when I entered the camp. But I didn't see my brother for three months, not until he was well, and I didn't know when I entered the camp that I couldn't leave. My three little kids were with my mother and had no food. But they wouldn't let me go back. They were afraid I would be killed. I was so angry.

One day I was sitting in the hut and crying. A husband and wife who were reporters came in and asked why I was crying. They might have been from Australia. The woman spoke Cambodian. The reporters tried to help me convince the authorities to let me go back, but they wouldn't let me.

I thought of escaping, but I didn't know the way. I was in Sakeo. It was the camp that helped you get to the U.S. more easily. A neighbor also wanted to run away from the camp. I said, "Do you know the way?"

"No," she said. "Do you?"

Neither of us knew the way so we didn't go.

I wanted to go to Khao-I-Dang, because from Khao-I-Dang I could sneak out to get my children. I put my name on a list to be transferred there, but my brother saw it and erased my name. I cried, cried and cried until my eyes swelled and turned black. I cried until I couldn't cry anymore.

My three children stayed with my mother. I did not see them again or know what had happened to them for six years, not until

1985. Two of them are married, but I never saw them again.

I could only reach Cambodia through my relatives in France, the Moa family, a husband and wife. Her mother lived in Cambodia. She asked her mother to look for my mother and mail any information to me. The only way you could reach Cambodia was through relatives in France.

The day I received the letter, I was home. I'd seen other letters from France, but when I opened it I saw it was from my mother and my children and I was so happy, I cried. In the letter, my mother asked when was I coming. She was getting old. Who would take care of the children? I really wanted to find a sponsor who would help my children to come to the U.S., but at that time, it was hard to find one. My mother was old and my sister, who lived with her too, was hard of hearing. I also had to have money to do it.

Now we talk by phone. From here to Cambodia it's five dollars for fifteen minutes. My brother will pay for me to visit there. My brother went to college and is a computer engineer. He lives in New Jersey, is married to an American and he has no kids. I still need money for when I get to Cambodia. Still, I plan to go next year in the summer.

My mother died in 1984. My uncle did not want to tell me directly. He wrote me a poem so I could interpret the meaning.

The first house I ever saw was my sponsor's house. I'd never been in a house like it. Everything was so new and clean. When I was in Thailand, people said that they'd have washing machines in the U.S. to wash your clothes. I said, who would make a machine that washed clothes? And I imagined a machine that looked like a person washing clothes like I did, with their hands. At the camp they said that in time, there'd be a machine made to feed you. I didn't believe there was a stove that had gas in it. When I first came here I didn't realize that toilets would be in the house. And I'd never seen a shower in a house either, only showers that were outside in a tent. I'd use the toilet by squatting over it instead of sitting on it.

The first time I saw snow, I was living in New Hampshire. I was riding a bike to Market Basket. I never thought snow would be so cold. If I'd known, I wouldn't have ridden the bike so far. But I got really hot from riding, so I took off my jacket, hat and shoes in the store. Everyone was staring at me.

When I got to the U.S., I noticed people put their hands in their pockets. I did not understand why they did this. I thought maybe they did it just to look cool. I realized later that it was just to keep their hands warm.

The sun doesn't seem like it comes from the same direction here. Does it rise in the same place? In Lowell it comes from a different place. In Boston it comes from someplace else. With the moon it's the same thing.

Sameth Chhang

Born 1954

We were a poor family. We had a house, a farm. There were no windows in the house. It was made of leaves from a thnot tree. The leaves are bigger than coconut leaves. If you walked into the house you would see a bag of rice. The bag was made from woven leaves. You would see a pail of water. The pail was the color of brick and made of clay. And you would smell the smell of cockroach urine. Outside in the rice fields, I would smell water and the fresh odor of the growing plants. I would think about how today I would have something to eat, but what would I eat the next day?

I went to school for three years. After school, I helped in the field. I planted rice. I picked out and squashed the bugs that destroyed the crops. I didn't play much because I was hungry. But when I did play, I used coconut shells. I put soil in the shells and poured in water and made believe I was cooking.

Seeds of Lotus: Cambodian and Vietnamese Voices in America

Duch Ouk

Born 1922

When I was eight years old, my mother took me to the temple to learn to read and write. There was no school then. I learned how to read the Sutra. I learned the alphabet. When my mother brought me into the temple, she told the higher monk that he could have all of our possessions in return for my education. All she wanted back were "my eyes and my bones".

The monk was my grand-uncle. He wore a yellow sarong, what monks still wear today. He was about sixty years old and he was very strict with the kids who didn't obey the rules. He had the right to whip me if I didn't do what he told me. The whip was made of thin bamboo. It was about the width of a finger and it was long and flexible, longer than my arm. It made a sound moving through the air.

One time I heard that there were all kinds of musicians playing, that there was going to be a celebration. But it was nighttime, time to sleep, and I couldn't go out and have fun. So three of us decided to sneak out by crawling through a toilet hole that led outside. But after the party, when we got back, we couldn't get in. The hole went out but it didn't go back in. So my friends and I ended up sleeping in the kitchen.

The cook found us and he told the monk to come see who was sleeping in the kitchen. The monk saw that it was the three of us there. Two of us got hit. Me and one other guy. My other friend ran away. The monk made me go find him, but by the time we came back, the monk had forgotten all about it.

Seeds of Lotus: Cambodian and Vietnamese Voices in America

 *Heng Sok*

Born 1924

My mother was very generous. The people in the neighborhood liked her a lot. She had nine children and I was the baby. Her face was long and she was tall and her skin was not too dark and not too light. Her name was Roo, which means "a life."

When I was four years old, I saw a hole that was narrow and deep. Kids dug them to trap crickets for their games, but I didn't know that then. I just wondered what was in the hole. I stuck my leg into it up to my knee and then I couldn't get it out. My mother ran over and she pulled me up too fast. She was afraid that something in the hole would hurt me.

She broke my leg and no one could fix it because there was no medicine. My mother felt so sad and sorry. She tried to find someone to help me. She called a spiritual doctor. But nothing helped. I've never been mad at her about it. She was so afraid. She wanted to save my life.

Seeds of Lotus: Cambodian and Vietnamese Voices in America

Sopheap Yin

Born 1956

There were eventually nine kids in my family and I was the first child. But when I was three months old, my mother and father threw me away in a forest. My father was a drunkard. My mother was young. My aunt picked me up though, and raised me until I was five years old. Then my mother asked to have me back. I thought my aunt was my mother and when I first met my mother I called her Auntie. I didn't know that I had brothers and sisters. My aunt gave me back.

When I lived with my real mother, I had five friends. Their names were Sam Bat, Sam Bo, Han, Mat Dao and On. My mother stored liquid cooking gas up high. One day I made a stairway so that I could go up and get the gas and all of us drank it. Then we drank a lot of water because we felt so hot, and then we all passed out. The neighbors found us and made us drink a sweet thick milk which gave us diarrhea and made the gas come out.

It turned out that my mother tricked my aunt. She only wanted me back so she could sell me to be a servant. She said she wanted me to play at my uncle's house, but I didn't want to go. She said I had to go to visit him because we were relatives, but when we got there, he wasn't at home. My uncle lived next door to the family who wanted to buy me.

When we arrived, it was 6 a.m. and the sun was already up. I remember that there was a big tree and a big rock. My mother left me at the rock and I sat there and I sat there, but no one came. I sat there until it was so dark, you couldn't see. Then the lady who bought me came. She told me my mother had sold me for 1000 riels.

The lady had a baby. I was five years old and she'd bought me to babysit for the baby. The family was wealthy, but they didn't treat me right at all.

They lived in a big house. The woman's name was Poy. Her husband's name was Natal. I lived in the kitchen. They put mosquito nets in there and right next to me, on the other side of the mosquito net, was a lot of food, fried bananas. I was very hungry, but I was afraid to take the food. The baby was with me and when the baby cried I hit it because I didn't know how to care for a baby. I hadn't eaten for a few days. Finally I made a hole through the net to eat the food and the lady found out and beat me.

They had a sixteen-year-old daughter. I don't remember her name, but she was tall and light-skinned. She had long hair and was pretty. I had to take her to school and I was only five. I washed her laundry. They would test me by leaving out money and food. They wanted to know whether I was bad or good. I didn't take the money, but their daughter took it. The money was gone and the mother asked the chauffeur to hit me with a ruler made out of metal. He hit me everywhere until I passed out. Then he poured water on me to bring me to, and then he hit me again.

The day after he beat me, the daughter confessed that she took the money. The mother said there was nothing she could do. It was too late. All she could do was say she was sorry.

Two days later, the daughter blamed a broken radio on me and I was beaten again.

When I was seven, I was still wearing the clothes I wore when I was five. At a factory nearby, they made gas and they used material to wipe their hands and when they threw it away, I took the material to make my clothes. I asked for a needle and thread from a neighbor, but I didn't know how to sew and sometimes the clothes would fall off me and I'd be naked.

My owner, Poy, said I could never go anywhere and the neighbors were of the higher class too and so I could never leave. I ran away once to my mother's but the soldiers came and took me back. My mother cried and held on to my leg to keep me. She was sorry she had sold me, but the soldiers said my mother had used her fingerprint, so it was legal, and my owner had the right to do anything she wanted with me. She even had the right to kill me.

For comfort I would go to a neighbor's house. The neighbors liked me. I was the youngest servant there. Sometimes I sneaked out to the school and stood outside the window of the classroom so that I could learn to read and write. Sometimes the kids would see me and say, "What are you looking at?" and throw things at me.

I stayed there until I was ten years old, until the war, when the Americans bombed in 1968. The owners had to leave to escape the bombing. They said, "We have to go. We have to pack."

I said, "No, I don't want to go." There were sacks of money there. The owners left the room for ten minutes and that's when I ran away.

I ran to a bus station. One of my uncles was there. He was a soldier. He said, "Why are you standing there?"

"Can you help me?" I said, "I have to get to my mom." She lived in Chamkar Leu.

My uncle asked the driver if I could get on the bus. He told him he would pay. The driver said, "Okay, if she can find a place to stand or sit." My uncle gave the driver about ten dollars to get me to my mother's house.

When I arrived, it seemed like no one had been there for a long time. The tiup fruit had fallen from the trees. The bushes had grown over the house so thickly I couldn't even get through them. Everyone who lived in the village was there, except my mother.

I lay down in the bushes around my house. My old five friends were still there and they saw me. They remembered me, but I couldn't remember them. I asked them if they knew where my mother was. "I came from the city, looking for my mom. Her name is Yin Kim," I said. My friends told me that my mother was at a farm which was very far away.

It took me from five a.m. to five in the evening to get there, running and walking all the way. I passed a lot of forests, and I didn't eat the whole day. I was afraid I would be caught, but because the country was under new rule, I was also hopeful something might have changed.

When I got there I saw my father. He was trapping fish in a stream. I said, "Dad! Dad!"

My father put his hand above his eyes and said, "Oh. Who is that?"

My father was eighty-five years old. He had cataracts in his eyes. My mother was half his age. By then, he had stopped drinking.

"Dad, it's me. Yin Yin," which was my real name. The Khmer Rouge changed my name to Sopheap.

"I can't see you," he said. "I can't hear you. Come closer." When he saw me he hugged me and cried.

He brought me to a small hut. I heard my mother running in the fields scaring the birds out of the crops. So I ran over to my mother.

I said, "Mom, do you know me?" And my mother ran to me and hugged me and we cried. I lived with my parents on that farm for five years.

Then one day when I was about sixteen, my mother had to go out in the fields again to scare the birds and she asked me to watch my baby sister, who was five years old. I needed to cook some rice, but I didn't have a light for the fire. I left my sister and ran around the village trying to find someone to give me a light. I was walking between a house and a fence when all of a sudden four men jumped from behind the fence, grabbed me and put me in a rice sack.

I screamed, "Help! Help me someone! Someone is kidnapping me!" I felt like I was suffocating.

One of them slung me over his back and walked. Then they put me on a wagon so they could hide me and travel farther. They let me put my head out of the bag so I could breathe. The men were about twenty-seven or thirty years old. They wore the black Khmer Rouge clothes and the red kerchiefs around their necks. The Khmer Rouge was not in power yet. They were not in the cities at the time, but they were wandering around the countryside kidnapping people. I didn't know of the danger, but others knew.

About halfway there, I saw a banana farm on one side of the road and an asphalt factory on the other. I said, "Can you release me? Can you bring me back home?" And they said, "We won't bring you back home because there is going to be a war in this country."

When we got to the place where there were others who'd been kidnapped, it was dark. The four men disappeared. Maybe they were the leaders. When I woke in the morning, I was told to go to the field. I was made to plant corn and beans. I made no friends there; I just worked. There was no time to make friends. When I went to sleep at night I felt I was never going to see my parents again. I would look around at the other people and watch them falling asleep and I thought, what if I tried to run away?

After a year, I did. I started at eleven at night. I walked and ran, walked and ran until six in the morning. I didn't know what to do; all I did was run. I heard scary birds around me, scary sounds, but all I could do was run.

Finally I saw a big highway. I stopped then and I didn't know what direction to take. I cried and cried and cried. I was lost. After I walked a little way, I saw a house. At least there was a house where I could go. I saw a village and walked there and into another village and I thought it looked like mine. It was my village Chamkar Leu. But I found my parents had moved away. The old people had moved out and new people had moved in. I asked the neighbors if they'd seen my mother. They told me my mother had moved to Phum O Da, a new village.

I went to the new village and there I found my parents. My father was still alive then. My parents had been looking for me for a year. They had not heard anything about my fate. But I was with them for only two nights. The four men found me again. They said to my mother, if you don't give us your daughter we will kill you. My mother said "My daughter's life has been so hard. Let her stay with me."

But they wouldn't. They took me. They said, "Either she comes with us, or she dies."

My mother said to me, "Don't worry. Some day we will see each other again. It has happened before."

This time they took me to a new place and they trained me to be a nurse. It was 1975 and the Khmer Rouge had taken over the country. In the new place, they taught me how to give shots and medication to people. A lot of people got sick from being moved to different parts of the country. I had never been in school and it was hard for me to learn. I didn't know how to read or write, so they taught me to memorize the different medications. I was willing to try, but it was so hard.

"If you want to live," they said, "You'd better learn. Otherwise you are no use."

I stayed in this new place for about a year and a half. I'd been trained in how to give shots and medicine, but then new rules came in and they decided that I was good for unloading rice from a ship on the Mekong River. They had separated the men and the women and I lived with about 200 women. We slept in hammocks on the boat and the leaders limited our sleep. When we heard the bell ring, we had to get up and start work. We ate flavorless soup made from rice and water. The people like me, who unloaded the rice from the ship then loaded it onto the trucks, were given better food than the others.

The ship was very big. We climbed 100 steps up and 100 steps down, then we had to walk across a long causeway from the ship to the dock. You could fall off on one side or the other into the water and a lot of people fell off and were killed.

One day the leader asked me where I lived. I lied. I told him I lived somewhere else because I knew the truck was going to Chamkar Leu. When I loaded on the rice, I also loaded blankets, medicine and other things for my mother. The truck traveled all night. I rode in the back with the rice. When we got there I asked the driver if I could see my mother. He said five minutes or else he'd get in trouble. I was so happy. I felt lighter. I screamed, "Mommy, I'm here!" But I only saw my sister. I asked her, "Where is Mom?" and she said they put her in another camp. It turned out that I never did see my mother again.

I asked my sister if she could deliver all my gifts to her, and she said yes. When I got back to the truck, the driver said we were all going to get into trouble because we were so late. When we returned, the leaders met with all the people on the truck. The leaders said I had lied and they said from now on I could not go to Chamkar Leu anymore. When we got back to work, they allowed other people to take breaks but I could not take any breaks and they did not allow me to carry rice anymore. Instead I had to carry empty gas tanks.

One day the bridge broke. It was the kind of bridge that bounced up and down when you walked on it. When it broke I didn't fall through. Instead it pushed me up and I got caught on it. I dropped the gas tank and the gas tank bounced and hit me in the head. There was blood everywhere. They just stitched it up and put me back to work.

In 1978 they moved me again, to Phnom Penh and they made me make clothes there for a year. The factory was in an old courthouse which had power there for the sewing machines. I made the black clothes for the soldiers. They had either a round neck or a collar. A lot of Cambodians dislike the color black. For three years, eight months and twenty days, we say, everyone wore black. No one cared about making friends. If you said something you could get in trouble. No one trusted anyone. You had to live day by day. I knew the country would never be the same again, but a few days before Vietnam took over, I prayed for things to get back to normal and to see my family again.

Three days before Vietnam took over, the leader of the sewing place said to me that I could pack. She said, "Take some rice and go to your mother." I hadn't known Vietnam was taking over. Only the leader told me.

I left the sewing place and saw people walking. I just followed them. I didn't know where my family was anymore. Some people wanted me to join the Khmer Rouge and fight. But I didn't. I followed people to the camp in Thailand. I trusted that someone knew the way. The journey took one year.

To get to the border of Thailand from Phnom Penh, you have to cross mountains and a river. A lot of people died from disease, from measles and from drowning in the river. I walked barefoot. I ate wild food. It was a rough life. Sometimes there were big trucks full of rice abandoned by the Khmer Rouge. But the Vietnamese would guard them. Once I stole some rice off a truck and I also caught a rooster. I had a bag of rice in one arm and a rooster in the other and was running. But I didn't see that there was a hole in front of me and I fell into it. The fall ripped off all my clothes. I ran back into the mountains and the Vietnamese soldiers shot at me. They would shoot at anyone who took the rice. Some died and some escaped.

After all the walking, my feet blistered and I was sick. I used my shirt to protect my feet. I crossed a mountain and looked down into a valley. It looked like it was burned, it was so hot. People lived in the valley, and I begged an old person for rice. I said I had no mother and no father and I was lost. The person was just about to give me the rice, but then someone said the Vietnamese soldiers were there, so I ran again for my life without the food.

The day I reached the border of the camp I saw the Red Cross giving out medication and food. The name of the camp was Sakeo II. There was a rumor that the Khmer Rouge lived in Sakeo II, but it wasn't true.

That was where I met my husband in1979. His name was Koasmoeung. A neighbor said he was a nice guy and he could take care of me. We fell in love. But we were not together long. I had my first daughter in 1980. My second daughter was born in 1983. When I was three months pregnant with my second daughter, he moved back in with his ex-wife. He never came back. I raised the two babies by myself. The last time I saw him, he was driving a truck out of the camp and he waved to me.

In 1985 I applied to come to the United States. I applied to a lot of countries, but only the U.S. took me. One day at the camp there was a giveaway of clothes and supplies. I asked a neighbor to watch my five-year old daughter, Yin Sophy, while I went to it. I took my younger daughter with me. It would have been hard to carry one and hold the other one's hand. When I came back I saw the neighbor's children, but I couldn't see my daughter. I said, "Sophy, Mommy's here. I have some clothes. Where are you?" I asked my neighbor, Sohen, "Where is Sophy?" She said, "They were playing. She was playing with my kids."

I looked in streams and holes and the public toilets, but I couldn't find her. The head of the camp helped me, the soldiers—everyone. Every day I went to the main office at 6:00 a.m. to ask them to help me find her.

Then I was chosen to come to the U.S., but I wanted to stay two more months to look for Yin Sophy. But the government wouldn't allow it. After her big sister disappeared, my younger daughter stopped eating and she was getting weak. They said they didn't have enough to help her here. "Do you want to lose two daughters?" they said, so I decided to go.

I believe my older daughter was kidnapped. I have never received any information about her since. She would be 21 years old now.

On the plane from Bangkok to the U.S., my younger daughter got very sick. She kept passing out and coming to. I screamed for help. I said, "My daughter is sick. My daughter is sick," but no one on the plane understood me. No one could speak Cambodian.

Finally, they landed the plane in Tokyo. They let me get off the plane first. They brought a stretcher out to the plane and I hopped on. I thought it was for me! They said, "Get off! Get off!"

There were a lot of police there. They surrounded me and they wore black uniforms, but I wasn't afraid of anything. I was just afraid for my daughter. I even hit a policeman. I said, "What are you doing?" Five men had to hold me down and calm me so they could help my daughter. When they took her in for x-rays, I said, "What are you doing? My daughter hasn't died yet." No was the only word I knew, so for three days and three nights, when someone asked me what I wanted to eat, all I said was no.

My daughter, Yin Sopan, stayed in the hospital for one week. They put her on an I.V. They asked me to stay with her. I lay down with her in the crib, and I was so tired I fell asleep and fell out of the crib onto the floor. I didn't even know I'd fallen out. The guy who lifted me back in told me.

At the hospital they called me to the phone and I didn't know how to use it. They'd found a translator who told me on the phone that my daughter was leaving the hospital and that we would continue our flight the next day to Minneapolis, Minnesota. It was 1986.

I was sponsored by Mary. Everyone knew her. And everyone knew Bun Li, who was the director of the Cambodian Mutual Association. They provided money, free food and free rent for the first three months in the U.S. Then the government provided financial help for the next two years.

When I got off the plane, I had one kid on my back and one kid in front, my son, who'd been born just before I left, and I carried one bag. I had no preparation. I saw snow coming down and said, "What's this? It's so cold."

My sponsor, Mary, couldn't find me. My hair was long, down to my knees, and it covered up my face. When she asked where I was, they said, "Look for the one with the real long hair and the two kids, one in front and one in back."

When I moved in to my sponsor's house, there were two separate beds, one for my kids and one for me. It was so nice that I was afraid I'd ruin it, so I slept on the floor instead.

One time Mary gave me money for the grocery store. I got ten cans of food and when Mary asked me what I'd bought I said, food in a can. All you have to do is open it and eat it. It turned out that I'd bought ten cans of dog food!

I had a very hard time learning to write my name. It took me four months with three or four people helping me. At the hospital, when they asked me what month I arrived in the U.S. I told them month fourteen. They said there's no such thing as a fourteenth month. I don't know my own birth date and every time someone asks me for information, I don't know it.

When my daughter left the hospital she was fine. We settled in Rochester, Minnesota and lived with a woman named Noam. One day I gave my daughter a bath, and afterward, I asked Noam's daughter to watch Sopan while I went to get a few things at the grocery store. By then, I had learned how to go shopping. I said, "Sopan is sleeping. Keep an eye on her in case she wants something." I was only going to be gone ten minutes.

At the store I didn't feel right. I thought there must be something wrong. I wanted to go home. Noam said, "We haven't even been here five minutes. We haven't gotten anything." So I stayed, but I didn't buy a lot.

When I got home, there were a lot of police at my house. I saw

Sopan with an oxygen mask over her face and fainted. I went to the hospital, too.

When I felt better, they told me I could speak to my daughter only five minutes. They had given medication to my daughter. I remember that my daughter, Sopan, just looked at me and shook her head.

Then they said she just passed away. No one knew why she died. She just went to sleep and went unconscious. The doctor asked for permission to find out why. He wanted to find out if it was her heart, but they never found anything wrong. I donated her heart for other people to use.

I still feel sorry now. I feel I should have never gone to the store. I should have never left her there.

My son is seventeen now and goes to Lawrence High School. He is a good son. He worries about me. He wants me to do anything I want. He says, "I'm going to get a good job and get a house and marry a girl who cares about you as much as I do." His name is Channy Yin.

After I was in the United States for two years, I paid a man to look for my mother in Cambodia. His name was Cum Stroung. He had a business in Cambodia, like a lost and found. You could pay him 100 to 500 dollars to look for your family. He only charged me 100 dollars and it took him four years. He found my mother in 1993. She lived at the very edge of Cambodia and he was afraid to go there to tell her where I was. He got to the town of Phum Ong and gave twenty dollars to another person to go and ask my mother if she would come to Phnom Penh to speak to him. She agreed to go and Cum Stroung videotaped my mother looking at pictures of me, so I watched my mother recognize me on the videotape. My mother said, "She is my daughter. We have been separated since the Khmer Rouge took over." Cum Stroung gave my mother twenty dollars for the trip back.

My mother asked my sister to call me. She didn't even want to know how I was. All she wanted was to ask me for money. I said, "If I hadn't found you, who would you ask for money? You, who sold me when I was little." I wanted her to at least ask how I was! She said she didn't want to talk about the past. She wanted to move on. But before

I sent her any money, I wanted to know why her nine other children were still with her and I was the only one she'd given away? I told her I had my own family to worry about. I had no husband and I didn't have money right now. About two months later I sent her $300. My mother sent me a video to thank me. She told me what my siblings were doing, how one was building roads, how one was a farmer.

But then my brother called and asked me for money to buy him some cows. I said, "If I had it, I'd send it, but remember that when Mom sent me away and I ran back, you hit me until my head bled." After that I stopped communicating with my family. My mother had used me all her life and she was using me again. I disconnected my phone.

Bo Toeur

My first wife died in 1975, when the Khmer Rouge took over. Her stomach got bigger and bigger and then she began to vomit blood. I was left to raise my five children alone. I was still in my home then. I lived in Banteay Srei. Then I moved to Aumal, where I was born. It was a village with huts made out of coconut leaves. There was only one room in the hut, and all the children slept in it together.

Before the Khmer Rouge, one thing I did was prepare bodies for cremation. When a body burns, it moves; it arches its back and opens its mouth. No one likes to see that. We bent the knees so that the feet were behind the back and then we tied the feet together. We crossed the arms over the chest. Then we wrapped the body in a rug, carried it on its back and flipped it over onto the wood so it lay on its stomach. We put wood over the body too, and sprayed water around the sides of the fire to make sure the body burned first. After the body had turned to ashes, we drew an outline of a person where the body once was. We drew a nose and a mouth and for the knees we used black rocks. We placed coins where the eyes once were. Then we put banana leaves on top. The A Cha, who is lower than a monk, would make a blessing over the body we'd drawn while touching it with the tip of a banana leaf. The ceremony is called Changing Bodies. It is to ensure that when we die we will come back again.

I also had my own land and house. I farmed rice fields, but when the Khmer Rouge took over they made me a fisherman. I fished with nets for food for the camp and I learned how to make the nets myself. I used threads from my own clothes and I used chain to weight the edges. I would find the chain myself or sometimes I would wrap plastic around rocks to weight the nets, too. If you gave me some nylon right now, I could make a fishing net. In the camp, the fish I caught was for everyone. If you took fish for yourself, they would kill you. But I would hide extra fish in the folds of my pants to give to my children.

One evening, around seven o'clock when it was still light, the leaders called a meeting. They asked who had kids seven years and older. They put the boys on one side and the girls on another. The children were quiet. My children were quiet, but they didn't know what was going on. I knew what was going on.

They took away my first three children. They left the last two, who were six and three years old, with me. The older three came to visit me every two months, or once a month if they lived close, and they would never want to go back. If they came to live with me, though, they would have had no food. We were only given enough to feed those who lived there.

After Vietnam took over, I sat in front of my house and waited for my children to come back. I saw a lot of my neighbors' children return and then I saw all three of my own. We were all united—Boun, my oldest daughter, Mearn, my son, and Mourn, my other son. I hugged them.

I left Cambodia because one of my daughters died of measles in 1979. She was five years old. I always felt I was missing one child and I couldn't forget it.

I wanted to leave Cambodia. If I stayed, I would have a hard life. I would have died of hunger or disease. My kids would not have been educated. There was no land.

I walked with my children and a thousand other people for three days and three nights to get to the camp called Khao-I-Dang in Thailand. We walked on one road and slept in the bushes. Beside the road were mines. I never saw one go off with my own eyes, but I saw a body.

Outside the camp it was empty. There was just red dirt and small bushes. They made a fence around the camp and there was a mountain on one side of it, too. We were on Chumrum Thmey at the border of Thailand. They took us into the camp in a big truck. When I first entered, the Red Cross provided food, bamboo sticks, and blue plastic to make a hut. I lived there one and a half months. I assisted the soldiers and I made chairs and tables out of bamboo. I was paid with chickens and vegetables.

In 1980, they asked the old ones to move and took us to Sakeo in a school bus. I made nets there. Then I went to the Island of Galang in Indonesia. It was eight kilometers square. There was a city in the camp, but I never saw it. There was water all around and it rained all the time, but there was no flood because the island was sand. A big boat provided food to this camp.

Meth and I were married in 1981, in the refugee camp. A friend of mine, named Phan, knew Meth and said to me one day, "Uncle, do you want to get married again?"

I said, "No, I'm too old." I was fifty-six at the time and Meth was twenty-eight. But my friend, Phan, kept coming back and would ask me again nearly twice a week, would I like to marry Meth. He felt sorry for her. She was an orphan with no one to depend on. Also, I had three sons to take care of on my own.

I kept saying no, until Phan came back and said, "Will you or won't you. Yes or no."

So I said, "Yes, if she'll take me." I still felt too old.

I'd never seen Meth before, but she'd seen me. So I took my sister and brother and went to Meth, and we arranged the marriage. All I could afford at the time was eight hundred bhat, some food and some traditional music. We had a traditional wedding at Sakeo.

I arrived in San Francisco in 1984. It was around two in the afternoon, in August. When we landed they gave us coats. We wore gloves, coats and hoods and we were still cold in August. Everything looked so different. The colors were so dark. Nothing was clean there. Everything was foggy. Even the smell was different, the way people dressed. We had to wear anything we could get, but people wore pants and shirts and shoes. Such nice clothes. The houses were so big. I noticed the chimneys because we don't have them in Cambodia.

The day I came to the U.S. was the day I arrrived in a new world. I didn't need to worry about hunger or being killed. I felt like I was going to live forever.

Seeds of Lotus: Cambodian and Vietnamese Voices in America

Kry Nhean

Born 1934

In 1975, I lived in Phum Yeang, on the border of Thailand. I was in my house when twelve Khmer Rouge soldiers arrived. They pointed machine guns at my back and ordered me to take them to the border of Thailand. I said, no. I was afraid to do it, because I was afraid that the Thai soldiers guarding the border would shoot me. But the Khmer Rouge soldiers said if I didn't, they'd shoot me anyway. They needed me to give them information about the border and the land, so that they could get into Thailand and trade gold for diesel. I figured I had no choice.

I walked in front of them, at gunpoint, from 6:00 a.m. to 6:00 p.m. Finally, we arrived at a sign that indicated the distance to the Thailand border. Then they ordered me to give them directions on how to mine and booby trap the area. They said the next day they would come back.

They returned with thirty more men and twelve trucks that carried all their supplies. Then they asked me to show them where to put the mines and the kind of booby traps that shoot spikes out of the ground when you step on them. I thought right then of running across the border to Thailand, but I knew they would kill me. I also had my five kids at home with my wife, Yin Seng.

The soldiers didn't go away. They kept coming until the place was full of them and they had turned the village into a camp. If they had not come, people would have run across the border.

During the day, my wife worked in the fields. They took away my two older sons to work with other kids their age, and I didn't know where they were. My job was to harvest nectar from a thnot or sugar palm tree. It's like a coconut tree. The men would climb the tree on a ladder and use a tool made out of bamboo or wood to pinch the stem of the flower. Then we would take a long, narrow bucket made from hollowed out bamboo, hook it onto the tree and let the nectar or juice from the flower drip into it all night. Then we climbed up the tree with empty buckets, unhooked the full buckets, replaced them with the empty buckets and poured the juice from the full buckets into a very big pot set over a hot wood fire in the middle of the village. The nectar would boil down into sugar. It would get very, very thick and when it cooled it hardened. The air always smelled of cooking sugar.

Before the Khmer Rouge came, I was a rice and banana farmer, but I also made the sugar from the thnot tree for my family or to sell at a market. I sold the sugar to make more money. I never knew what the Khmer Rouge did with it.

My family and I continued to live in Phum Yeang for five months. Each night hundreds of people tried to cross the border and were killed by mines. I would hear the explosions because the border was only two miles away. And every time the Khmer Rouge trapped them, they would kill them. If anyone fell in love, they killed them too by cutting their throats. But for the first five months there was enough food.

Then one day the Khmer Rouge announced over a loudspeaker that everyone should leave. They said if you want to stay, then stay. But they didn't say if you stay you will be killed. Three families stayed and they were killed. The whole village, 488 households, were forced to leave. The Khmer Rouge made us go to Phum Kouk. It took a whole day and night to get there. Phum Kouk was just empty land, so on the first night we slept on the ground. The next day I collected leaves and small bushes and the commander told everyone to make the same house. They made people go back to Phum Yeang, destroy the houses there and take the metal to use for roofs of the houses in Phum Kouk.

I was very angry that I had to leave my old home, but I had to do it to survive. My sons, though, were at the new place and that made me happy, but they were only there for two weeks. Then they were taken somewhere else. Now life got harder. I was separated from my wife and they took my daughter, Sor, away to a separate camp. She was fourteen. My wife was with the two younger children.

There, I made houses and waterwheels and I lived only with men. I ate two small bowls of rice a day. People were ill from hunger and disease. At Phum Kouk, they turned people against each other by making us guard each other. People would turn each other in. If the people who were guards did not make those they were watching work hard enough, the Khmer Rouge would kill them. They killed twelve in one day.

When they wanted to kill someone they called a meeting. One day they called a meeting at about 5:00 p.m. They were going to execute a man because he had been a soldier who fought against the Khmer Rouge. His name was Seang. The first I heard of him was when I had to watch him be killed. They tied him to a tree and made us sit on the ground around him while the Khmer Rouge stood behind us to make sure everyone watched. They explained why they were going to kill him. Then they took an axe. They cut open his back and skinned him like a fish. Then they reached in and pulled out his gall bladder.

A week later a man named Phal died the same way. I didn't see it with my own eyes, but I heard that Phal said, "Why are you killing me? My mother is old. No one can take care of her. You should kill us both." So they did. The Khmer Rouge planted a coconut tree over both the bodies. I don't know why.

They put me in charge of a group of people, too. One person ran away, so the Khmer Rouge blamed me. They said I hadn't watched closely enough and put me in a special prison camp. There, they chained both my arms by the wrists. They gave me a teaspoon of water to drink and a bowl of rice to eat a day. All you did was wait day by day, month by month, to die. Every night they tied a hundred prisoners to a rope and led them out. They were only skin and bone. They had no energy left to fight, and they never came back.

I was there for one year. Then it was my turn to be taken out to die. There were ten of us. They took the nine men before me and then a Khmer Rouge soldier said, "Let me kill this man myself." His name was Phong Soung. I knew him from before. We fought as soldiers together against the Khmer Rouge. I thought he was going to kill me for sure.

I said, "Go ahead and kill me. I don't want to live like this anymore." After I said that, Phong Soung started to cry. He pulled me up and put a knife to my throat, but he cut his own arm instead. He took my shirt, wiped his blood on my shirt and put my shirt on a tree. Then he put a gun behind my head and shot the gun four or five times, but he didn't shoot me. Other Khmer Rouge saw what he had done, but they didn't stop him. I thought, why is this guy not killing me?

Then he put me on his motorbike and drove me out of the camp and to a house in Pailin where some people took care of me. I stayed there for one week. After starving for so long I ate and ate and ate. When they took the food away, I wept. Phong Soung gave me a letter and told me to show the letter to people, that it would make me safe. He had asked the man who cared for me to take me to Phnom Aoral.

Phnom Aoral was another prison and so the Khmer Rouge still kept an eye on me. I had to stay on a mountain and I could not come down. I had better food there though. That was where the Khmer Rouge wanted me to marry again. I said no. I said, "I'll only do it if I can see my family again." So the head of Phnom Aoral wrote a letter that allowed me to travel to my family. They took me there by truck, accompanied by three Khmer Rouge soldiers, to make sure I didn't run away.

But when I reached the village, my wife and children weren't there. I was afraid. I thought they'd been killed. But the people in Phum Kouk told me that the Khmer Rouge had made them move to Phum Run, which was fifteen kilometers away. I walked all day, from 6:00 a.m. to 3:00 p.m., and when I arrived, I asked the people there if they'd seen my family. Then I saw them. My wife and my two younger children were boiling tadpoles over a fire. All that was left of them was skin and bone. I couldn't speak. I started to cry. My other two children were there too, but my older son had been forced to marry.

I told the Khmer Rouge soldiers, "Now you can see that my wife and my children are still alive. You can tell your leader to kill me, but I'm not going back. I'm going to stay with my family."

I felt terrible for my wife. She had not been treated well by the people there. They said she was an outsider because she had come later. They said she was eating their food. I went to the leader and asked for a job. They said there was no place for me on the farm, so I went back to making sugar from the sugar palm tree. I stayed there until Vietnam took over. When they took over, they bombed a village instead of the city and that is how my son's wife died. She was four months pregnant. After the Vietnamese took over, I went back to my old village.

The Khmer Rouge and Vietnamese were fighting around the village and the Khmer Rouge forced me to leave the village and go to Phum Sangh. I lived in Phum Sangh for three months. Then, after Vietnam took control of the country, I moved back to Phum Run. My whole family was there with me, my wife and five children, but we could barely survive. We ate once a day—rice with a little watercress.

We were starving, so we left at the end of 1978. We went to the Thailand border, to Chumrum Thmey, and lived there for two months. I sold water to support my family. The water hole was far away, two miles. I carried it in two buckets attached to the ends of a bar I'd lay across my shoulders. By the time I got back, most of the water had spilled.

You could buy equipment, like the water buckets, with gold. The gold was in the form of jewelry, gold chains that you cut into small pieces. People had hidden their jewelry inside the seams of their clothes. I sold sugar I'd made from the sugar palm tree to get gold. Those who couldn't trade with gold, hollowed out bamboo stalks and made buckets from those.

At the border, everyone tried to run across to Thailand, but people were killed. After the two months at Chumrum Thmey, we moved to Nong Chan. I used the money I'd made selling water to buy ingredients to make and sell cakes. I also sold cigarettes and sweet rice. All my children helped me. We lived there for two weeks. The war was going on between the PARA, the Cambodian fighters who were not with the Khmer Rouge, and the Thai soldiers. Everywhere people were dying. You could hear the screaming and I saw people hit by shells. I was in the middle of a battle that occurred over one day and one night.

Finally, I moved across the border to Thailand. We walked with a lot of people and got across without getting shot. Then, on December 4, 1979, the Red Cross arrived with twenty trucks, the kind that transported soldiers. They'd come to take us to the refugee camps and to get all of us there, all twenty trucks had to make eight trips. I knew the trucks had come to help us, but the PARA didn't want us to get on. The United States Red Cross would say, "Get on! Get on!" but the PARA would put guns to people's heads and threaten to kill them to get them to stay and fight against the Thai.

I was lucky. I got my wife and children on the first truck on the first trip. I got on the second truck and we arrived at the camp at the same time.

The first camp we went to was Sankat Pram at Khao-I-Dang. There was nothing there but an empty field. The Red Cross provided us with ten bamboo poles for the frame of our house and a blue tarp, for a temporary roof. They gave us shovels to dig the holes for the four poles that made the corners. Then we slanted two across the top and attached them with rope, which they also provided. Later on, the Red Cross brought us fronds from the sugar palm tree to lay across the top, and we made the floors by criss crossing bamboo. My job was to make five houses a day. I worked with twelve people and made five houses a day for ten years. I also made a hospital, a school, a temple and an orphanage. Two hundred of us would also leave the camp each day to build houses for people outside of it, and then we'd return to the camp at night. The head of the camp wanted to keep me there to keep building, but I left for the United States in 1989.

I didn't want to stay. I wanted to move on. I wanted to go forward. It wasn't safe there. PARA soldiers robbed people in the camps and sometimes raped the women. My wife, children and I were glad to leave. We spent one night in Tokyo, then flew to San Francisco, and then we arrived in Boston.

Seng Yin

Born 1935

In 1976, three of my children were taken from me and two stayed with me. It was hard because of the starvation. The potato skins I boiled gave me and my children diarrhea. The neighbors gave me some soup and a little medicine. I fed it to my two children and kept some for myself and got a little bit of energy. My son's hair fell out in clumps.

Mr. Kry and I were separated in 1978. My older son was forced to live with his group. He would steal some corn and fish and bring it to me. My older daughter brought us husks of rice, normally something we'd feed to the pigs. When I came to the U.S. I had surgery because the rice husks were still in my intestine.

One day my daughter was so hungry, she snuck into a corn field and picked baby corn for us. The leader caught her and tied her hands. I begged him. "Don't kill my daughter," I said. "This is only the first time, so spare her." The leader said if it happened again, then all of us would die.

My second son was caught stealing pumpkins. They called us all together, stood my son in front of us, tied his hands behind him, hung the pumpkin from his neck and pointed a gun at his head. They said if they saw his mother cry, they would kill him. I covered my eyes, but they didn't know I was the mother. They weren't really looking for me, but I was afraid they would know. I'd seen them kill a whole family in front of the group.

One day they called the families to get food and on the way, I fell. I was too weak and tired to get up out of the mud. My children sat beside me and cried. The people who came after me stopped and helped pull me out. The children and I hadn't eaten for a week. All we could have was three small pieces of potato. If you worked, you ate. If you didn't work, you didn't eat. I was too weak to work.

We had no clothes, just little pieces of cloth to cover our private parts, no shoes. We would find leaves to cover ourselves. We'd use vines to hold them on.

When Mr. Kry came things got easier because he could work. I hadn't seen him for two years and didn't know if he was alive. He brought potatoes and we cooked them and ate. He missed our kids so much he grabbed them and my younger daughter said, "Mommy, Mommy, there's an old man grabbing me and I don't know him."

The youngest was three and when she ate after starving for so long, she didn't stop. Then she couldn't get her breath and started sweating and she couldn't close her eyes. She started to go unconscious. In Cambodia, if you overeat, you make a gesture with your hand that's like pushing something away and say "Take it out, take it out, take it out." I did it three times for my daughter and she recovered.

I already knew how to weave and in the refugee camp I wove rugs. I'd been taught a long time before. I wove five rugs a day and once a month I'd get a chicken and some clothes. I'd leave for the rug factory at 8:00 a.m., then come home to make lunch for me and my two youngest children. Then they went back to school and I went back to the factory until four or five in the evening.

Mr. Kry and I grew up in the same village. One day when I was eighteen and he was nineteen, we were working in the rice fields together and we decided to have a race: who could plant the field faster. Then we started pulling out the grass and spraying each other with the muddy water on the roots. Still, I didn't fall in love with him. Every time I saw him I wanted to swear at him. My mother didn't want me to be with him either. His father had a lot of wives, and we were afraid he'd be the same way.

I remember another day, though, I was walking down a path carrying water in two clay buckets that hung from a pole across my back. Mr Kry was hiding in the bushes and when I passed him, he pulled me into the bushes. I pushed him away and sent him flying, then I hit him with the water buckets and both of them broke. But Mr. Kry won, and that was the day I fell in love with him.

I was so late in coming home that my parents asked everyone to go out and look for me. Mr. Kry took me to his stepmother's house. He said we had agreed to be together, so his stepmother went to my house. She said to my mother that we ran away together and we should get married right away. The belief is that if you don't get married before you sleep together you can have a curse put on you. But my mother said, no. She said, "In order for me to give my daughter to you, you must provide us enough *sra* for one hundred people." *Sra* is a special wine that comes in an enormous clay container. It's about one hundred proof alcohol. She also asked for cakes and cookies and fruits and 5000 riels. She wanted to make it very hard for Mr. Kry to marry me.

Mr. Kry, though, owned cows that he used for farming. He had been making his own living since he was ten, when his mother died. He sold three of them and he also made money by selling sugar he made from the sugar palm trees. He made 5000 riels from the cows and 1000 more from the sugar. It took him a month. When he returned to my house with the wine and cakes and money, the celebration began. Mr. Kry provided the wine, but my family, the girl's family, has to provide the food, and sometimes families hire a special chef for 300 riels to do the cooking. The celebration went on for two days and one night, and people danced the whole time.

Seeds of Lotus: Cambodian and Vietnamese Voices in America

Phay Seang

Born 1947

My mother had nine children, six sons and three daughters. I am the eighth child. My mother sent me to the temple to learn to read and write, but when I was ten, my older brother said he wanted me to be part of his family. My brother vowed that if I would look after their children, when I grew up I would have part of his land. We set out candles and incense and we prayed in front of the shrine three times. He said, "If I break my promise, I will die before the age of fifty."

My brother broke his promise. He refused to give me part of his land because I married against his wishes, and my brother died when he turned fifty. His wife took over the family, and I moved out when I was twenty, in 1967. My brother lied. He took me from the temple and if he had not taken me when I was ten years old, I could have learned to read and write. I am still angry at him now.

Before he died, he told me to go live in Phum Snoeng and take the land for myself. It was one kilometer from his house. It was like a ghost town. At night I could hear screaming. It was haunted and I heard that it had been a burial ground. But there was nothing I could do. I had to live there from 1967 to 1970 to support my family. During that time I had three children.

The Khmer Rouge had not taken over the whole country yet, but they were taking over the land far outside of the cities. If you went west, you'd be in Khmer Rouge country. If you went east you'd still be in free country. They came one evening at 5:00 o'clock when I had just climbed the sugar palm tree to switch the buckets. They pointed their guns at me and said, "Come down right now!" They ordered the whole area, about three hundred households, to leave and move to the mountains. They said, "If you don't leave on this day, we will kill you."

When we reached the mountains we had to cut the trees to make a clearing and make our huts. The Khmer Rouge was in charge. They divided us into different groups. One group farmed rice, another farmed potatoes, another different vegetables. All the food was put together and rationed out, but there was not enough. Many people tried to escape. If a hundred tried to escape, two succeeded, the rest were killed.

I lived there for two years, from 1972 to 1974. In 1974 I became very ill. I had a high fever and I was unconscious from three in the afternoon until ten the next morning. I couldn't move or speak, but I could hear what everyone was saying. They were saying that I was dying, but I could not awaken to speak, myself.

They prepared to have me buried. My wife put me in a hut and covered me with a white blanket. When my sister-in-law came to take a peek at me, I said, "Sister, can you make me some rice soup?" She thought she had seen my ghost! She ran to get my father-in-law. She thought I was a spirit and she said they should bury me right away. I said I hadn't died, that I was just too weak to get up. After my sister-in-law gave me the rice soup I was better.

During the nineteen hours I was unconscious, I had a spiritual experience. A spirit took me to what looked like a castle and there was a king there. His name was Cho Da Kresiem. He asked me what my name was.

I said "Phay Seang."

He said, "How many children do you have?"

I said, "Five children."

The king opened a book that told him the dates of everyone's birth and death. He said, "You can go back home now. The spirit took the wrong person." And he said, "A lot of people are going to die. And you are going to die, but again, you will come back to life." When I woke up another person in the camp died.

At the end of 1974, the Khmer Rouge told us we had to move again. They put new people in our camp and we went to Phum Thnaot. I lived there in the beginning of 1975. By now the Khmer Rouge had taken over the whole country.

Then the entire village moved to Phum Rohal. The Khmer Rouge forced me to be a fisherman. I had only fished when I was younger, but now I had more responsibility. They separated me from my wife and I fished with the other men. My wife worked with the women. The children were with my wife and we never saw each other. The food was pretty normal, soup in the morning, more to eat at night. Because of Cambodia's history, I believed that there would be someone who would come in the future to help us, who would conquer the Khmer Rouge and take over Cambodia. Those who were able to hear a radio believed we would be saved. Those who didn't hear anything from the outside believed we would have to live under the Khmer Rouge forever and did not have any hope.

I began to die again in 1976. Food was getting shorter and shorter. You would mix a little rice with part of a banana tree, maybe some potatoes, to make it thicker. I got sick with a high fever again from not having enough to eat, so they put me in a cart and pushed me to the hospital. My wife wanted to go with me, but they wouldn't let her.

I stayed in the hospital for a month and a half. The hospital was clean, but no one talked to me. After I was there a week, they were ready to put me where all the dead people were. My fourth brother was there too. He'd had an operation for a hernia and he had recovered enough to be given the job of carrying the dead out for burial. The doctor said, "Mr. Phay has died. Bring him out and bury him."

I was really unconscious though, and I talked aloud. I said I haven't died yet. I said that the Vietnamese were going to take over the country. They thought I was a spy working for Vietnam, but my brother said to the doctor, "He's just a fisherman. He doesn't know anything."

When I was dying, I was visited by a spirit. The spirit was an old man who told me the future. He said I would not stay in the same place. He said, "Don't worry. Everyone will travel to the West."

The doctor gave me shots every morning to make me better and give me energy. The doctor was an average-looking man, but he'd been hit with a piece of shrapnel in one eye, so one eye was blind. When he gave me the shot, the needle wouldn't go into my skin, so the doctor thought I might be one of those people who no one can shoot or kill. He said, "We don't want people like you around. We will kill people like you, who can predict the future. I will give you three chances. If the first, second and third shot won't go through your skin, I will kill you."

The first shot did not go through. Before the second shot, the doctor called in a lot of soldiers who stood around to watch. They said, "Why are you so tough? We can't do anything to you."

One soldier, who was about my age, stepped forward and slapped my face. He said, "The next time he can't give you the shot, we're going to kill you."

The doctor asked my brother how I got this way and asked if I had read any book to become this way. My brother said I hadn't. The second shot did not go through either. I prayed for the third shot to go through and I hit both arms three times. The third shot went in.

My brother asked Mr. Ung, an old man, my uncle, to protect me by giving me a medicine so I wouldn't see the spirits anymore. Mr. Ung made a special medicine of a blackened wood which he scraped and mixed with water. After I drank it, all the spirits disappeared. But I remembered what the spirits told me: that we had to escape to the West, that there will be a lot of problems, a lot of death, but if we went to the West we would survive.

In 1977 the Khmer Rouge forced us to go west by relocating us to Ampil Pram Dern. In one month, two of my three daughters and son died of hunger and disease. We could not have the monks pray for seven days and seven nights before we buried them, which is the tradition, but we could bury them ourselves.

I had two children left, a son and a daughter. When we arrived, my daughter was trained to be a nurse, my wife and younger son were made to cook, and I was a farmer. We were separated again.

In January of 1978, I fell asleep at the foot of a small hill. In my sleep I saw an old man on the hilltop. He said, "Why are you still sleeping? There are Vietnamese all over the place in Phnom Penh. If you go," he said, "go to the west."

I woke up at four a.m., but I waited until seven to run over to where my wife worked. I said to her, "Prepare to go because Vietnam has taken over."

The leader there said, "Why are you going to get your wife?"

I said, "If you have a radio, turn it on and you'll know."

The leader said, "If it's not on the radio that Vietnam took over Phnom Penh, I'll shoot you."

When the leader heard the news, he was scared and wanted to save himself. He asked which way he should run. I said, "If you run to the east you will get killed." So a lot of Khmer Rouge soldiers ran to the west too. Anyone who ran east was shot by the Khmer Rouge.

Then I went to the hospital where my daughter worked. My daughter said, "How do you know they've taken over?"

I said, "Do you want to stay or go?"

So my daughter packed to go.

At the Thailand border, because of the hunger, the Cambodians sold anything, cows, clothes, everything they had, to buy food to eat. Men and women tried to cross to steal corn, and many people were killed by mines and bamboo booby traps. The Thai soldiers shot people, too. I saw people die in front of me. I lived on the border for a year. Many people died because Thailand would not let us cross the border. Then one day the Red Cross came and spoke over a megaphone. They said other countries are opening their borders to you. If you want to go to a third country (first was Cambodia, second was Thailand and third was a country like the United States) we will take you to Sakeo I.

After one week there, my wife became very ill. She went to the hospital at the refugee camp. I left my six-year-old son with my daughter and went to the hospital to see her. My wife gave me a tangerine and an egg to take back to our son. When I gave my son the tangerine, he took one small bite and he died right away. I carried him to the hospital and they gave him a shot of a dark liquid. He moved his fingers a little bit, but he died. I couldn't bury him. The Thai took him away and buried him.

I was with my wife and daughter at Sakeo I for six months. Then we traveled in a cart pulled by cows to Sakeo II. Then I moved to Khao-I-Dang, where I helped build a canal system for washing and bathing water. We were paid for our work with chicken, soy sauce and clothes. In the refugee camps I made friends. We could talk and tease each other. We could say what we wanted.

At Sakeo II, after my son died, I asked my wife if I could marry another woman because I had no son to carry on my name. My wife said yes, and she left and went back to Cambodia. Her own family was in Cambodia. My daughter married and had her own children.

The first time I saw Voeun, she was taking a shower. I told her she was pretty. I said, "There's a good vegetable over there to eat." Voeun took me seriously and said yes, there are good vegetables to eat. Then I said, "What about sleeping with that vegetable?" Then Voeun started to catch on.

Voeun did not have any parents, so I asked the elders if I could marry her. They gave me permission. We married in 1980. I was thirty-three and Voeun was twenty-three. We had two daughters at the camp; we've had six children altogether.

After Khao-I-Dang, we went to Chonburi. Then we spent one year in the Philippines. While I waited, I only worried about how I was going to use the toilet. I still use a toilet by squatting over it! I wondered how I was going to turn the water on and off.

A lot of people returned to Cambodia because they lost all hope of leaving, but we arrived in the U.S. in 1986.

Before we got on the plane, we all had to take off our clothes and they inspected us from head to toe. They tapped my penis with a pen. I think they kind of did it as a joke, to see if I'd get bigger and then they laughed and let me go. I wanted to say, the thing's asleep now, but if it gets mad, you're in trouble!

Before I got on the plane, they gave us bread. I saved it because I didn't know if there'd be food on the plane. They had to step on the bread to keep me from taking it. The translator told me I'd have more to eat on the plane.

When I was on the plane I was really afraid it would fall. I held on tight, especially sitting by the wings. Then I went to the bathroom and there was a man in there with me. I said, "Why are you looking at me?" and I swore at him. He wouldn't go away, so finally I just peed, and when I shook myself, I saw that the guy shook too, and that was when I realized it was my reflection. I'd never seen a mirror before. I'd never seen myself.

Nikki Toeur

Born 1966

I was born June 5, 1966. I grew up in a small valley called Botangsoue, where I lived with my older half-sister, my mom and my dad.

One time, I believe it was in 1971, I remember I saw my mom crying and I looked inside of the house and saw my dad lying down flat on the bed. The bed was made out of bamboo and he was covered up with a white blanket. I saw four monks blessing him and those who lived in the Botangsoue valley were there too. I asked my mom, "Mommy, what's wrong with my dad and why are a lot of people here?"

My mom told me that my dad was no longer with us anymore. "He went far away," she said, and she cried. A few months later, I asked my mom again about my dad. This time she told me that my dad had passed away.

My dad worked in a mine for precious stones and when he was alive, we didn't have to worry about anything. But after he died everything started to slow down. We were short on money, and my mom became sick. My sister had to go out and find a job to support my mom and me. Luckily she got a job as a housekeeper.

My sister also met her husband, who worked as a driver. They got married in 1974. She and her husband stayed in Botangsoue, while my mom and I moved to Pailin and started a new life. My mom got a job working as a housekeeper for some very rich people. He was an army commander. I was eight years old and I helped my mom with babysitting at the commander's house. The family was very nice. They always took us with them wherever they went.

It was about 7:00 a.m. on April 13, 1975. My mom and I went over, as usual, to work at the commander's house and we found that the door was open, but no one was there. My mom and I wondered where they'd gone. We kept going back, but no one was there.

On April 17, I got up in the very early morning, and I heard bombing and shooting and also heard the voice of a Khmer Rouge soldier. He told us to go southeast. He said he would kill anyone who didn't follow his orders.

My mother carried about fifteen pounds of rice and some clothes. I helped her by carrying some dried fish, dried beef, some salt and some water. As time went by, my mom and I ran out of food and dry meat. We didn't need to worry about water, though. There was a flood. Everywhere we went we came back wet. Water was everywhere.

At about noon, I saw a Khmer Rouge commander who told us that we had to stop where we were and make our own house to live in and find our own food to eat. We saw a small dirty barn, a very old barn that had been left there a long time. We were lucky. We got there before everyone else. My mom and I cleaned it and we lived there for about three months. We had no food left. We had nothing. The clothes we'd taken we had traded for food. My mom would sneak to Phnom Sampeau to trade gold for rice and would have to leave me alone in the barn for three or four days. If she hadn't, we would have starved. It was lonely with nothing to do, wondering where my mother was. But she was lucky. She came back each time.

One day my mom took me with her from Bang Krasar to Phnom Sampeau. It takes about three days. When we got to the Phnom Sampeau Temple, I saw a lot of monks and nuns. I remember my mom asked one of the nuns if we could have some food and stay for the night. We left the next morning and got to Khum Chrey at 5 p.m. My mom asked the mayor if we could stay there.

"Where did you come from and why did you come here?" he said.

My mom told him we came from Bang Krasar. "We have no food to eat, no place to live."

"Okay," he said. "You can stay here if you work for us and we will look after you everywhere you go. But if you do something wrong or you don't listen to what I say, I will make you and your daughter go to sleep and never get up."

About five months later, at about seven in the evening, the group leader called a meeting. He said that children seven years old and up will be separated from their parents to help with farming. I was a kid and I thought it would be fun to meet a lot of kids the same age and make a lot of friends.

After about two days, though, I started to miss my mom and began to cry. I asked the group leader if I could go back home. She said no. She told me I could not see my mom. So I told her that if she didn't let me go see my mom I would run away that night. After hearing that, she tied me to a tree and left me there overnight without any food. When she released me the next morning I was sick from missing my mom and from having not eaten for almost two days. The group leader asked a kid to go tell my mom that I was sick.

A few hours later I saw her. I got up out of the bed and hugged her and said, "Mommy I miss you and I want to go with you when you go to your place." And I told her what they did to me. She started to cry and she said I could not go with her. She said if I went with her we would both get killed. They let my mom stay with me the full day. She left at 6 p.m.

I had a friend there named Eng. We would cry together and say we missed our moms, but she was too afraid to run away with me. So I ran on my own to see my mother two times, but I had no luck. They caught me both times. They tied me to a tree and put poison ants on me so I got a rash all over my body. They hit my shins with wooden boards so my legs would swell up. I knew I wouldn't be able to take it much longer, so I started to listen.

They told us we could see our parents once a year, on New Year's. So when New Year's came, I said, "I want to go see my mom." But they told me I had to stay and cook. New Year's came and went.

My mom had said to me if someone else takes over the country, I should meet her in the first place we'd arrived, Khum Chrey. So, in 1978, when the Vietnamese took over, I ran there and I asked an old lady, "Auntie, did you see my mom?"

"She waited and waited," she said. "Then she got sick. Then she went to look for you."

"She never came," I said. "I just came from there." I waited and waited. Then I went back again to where I'd been but nobody was there. It turned out that I never saw my mother again.

The old lady said I shouldn't stay there alone, so I lived with her until a man came to the village and said he was my uncle. He asked me, "What's your dad's name?"

I remembered they called my father Akul, which is a nickname. When you're dark-skinned in Cambodia, that's what they call you. My uncle knew the nickname.

My uncle had five smaller children, and he asked the lady if I could come and live with him. "Are you sure she's your niece?" she said. She wanted him to take good care of me. She was very nice, but she had a daughter and a son and I was afraid of the son. I was afraid he would flirt with me, and I did not want to do anything wrong. My uncle assured her that I was his only niece. I chose to go with him because he was my uncle.

He had a horse, so he'd traveled far and brought me back with him. I lived with him in Sisophon. From there, my uncle would travel to Thailand, get food from a farm and bring it back. This was 1979. I was too young to travel with him and I was a girl, so I would help sell the food he brought back from the border.

Every day was a struggle. First we had three meals a day, then we were down to two, then one. We would take rice and mix it with everything to feed the four or five of us in the family. No more gold, no more rice, so my uncle sold the horse for two ounces of gold. He said if we stayed there, we would die from starvation. We had to run to the border town, to Thailand. It took three days and three nights. Not long. I carried the baby and she never cried.

On the way, people stole from each other. My uncle would try to scare them away by saying, "The Khmer is right over there. Run!" The whole way was booby-trapped. There were mines. People would step on them and be killed. I never saw bodies though. I heard the shooting and the explosions.

My uncle didn't have much rice left and he had to give one cup to someone who would take the younger children across a river in a boat. The water came up to my chin. We had no dry clothes to get into and we had nothing on our feet. Our feet started to blister and bleed. I hit something with my toe and my toenail came out. I remember how much it hurt.

We got to Chumrum Thmey where my uncle traded two ounces of gold for food. We lived there for two or three months. We had to go a mile and a half away to collect water. By the time we returned the water was almost gone. My health was good, but I had pinkeye all the time. There were no bathrooms, so there was human excrement everywhere. I'd wake up and there'd be some by my head. A lot of people died there from disease. More people kept coming and coming. Then everything got hard again. We went from three to one meal a day again.

We were still not in the camp. My uncle's friend worked for the French Red Cross. He told us that in one week there'd be a truck to take people to the Khao-I-Dang camp. He said one truck would go to the camp and one would go to the border of Thailand. The Vietnamese didn't stop us from going. They didn't care if we left Cambodia. They probably wanted us out so they could take over.

I met up with my half-sister in Chumrum Thmey and found out that her first husband had died and the Khmer Rouge had married her to someone else. My uncle said I could live with them, but I didn't trust my sister's husband. He had too many girlfriends. He was too eager to have me stay with them. I loved my sister a lot but I didn't trust my brother-in-law. I was too scared.

We got on the truck. My uncle's sister did not come with us. She went back to Cambodia.

Khao-I-Dang was just an empty place surrounded by mountains. The ground was red and covered with cut down bushes. It looked pretty. We had to make our houses.

I was around thirteen years old. Every morning I climbed up the mountain to find wood to make a cooking fire and help my uncle's wife make flat noodles. Then I'd go from house to house to sell them. Sometimes my uncle crossed the refugee camp border to get cucumber, which he'd bring back for me, my uncle's wife and her two other daughters to pickle with bean sprouts, *san dek ban doh*, and sell in small bags.

In the camp, I attended school for five months, but the government only provided us rice to eat so I had to go to work to earn meat. I missed school and would watch the other kids playing when I was selling food, but my uncle had too many kids. Two were my age and had the chance to go to school, but maybe they were too lazy. I really wanted to learn. But I didn't blame my uncle. We had to make a living.

We were there almost a year. Then, when new people moved in, they made the old refugees move out to Sakeo I. Life in Sakeo was more fun after I met my old friend Eng. I met her at the place we got water. I remember we looked at each other. And then I called her name. We cried and hugged.

She said, "Where's your mom?"

I said I'm not with my mom. She cried and hugged me again. She was with her mom, her dad and her sister. I told her I was with my uncle.

"I never knew you had an uncle," she said.

I said I hadn't really known either. "But he's my uncle," I said.

Eng was the only friend I had in the camp. Eng's mom and dad were very nice and knew their daughter had to go to school. Eng asked if I wanted to go. But I had to do the housework; then I had to start the cooking. Then I could go to the schoolyard to play. But I also had to take care of my uncle's youngest one who was five months old. My uncle worked at the soldier camp for food and clothes and my uncle's wife helped hand out food in the camp. When the daughter wanted milk I would run her down there so my uncle's wife could nurse her. The two older daughters didn't help out with the youngest because they knew I would.

Again, every time new people came to camp, people had to move to the next camp. At the end of 1981 we moved by bus with about one hundred families to a new camp in Thailand. I lost touch with Eng. There were a lot of refugee camps in Thailand. The new camp, Mai Rut, was a very nice place. Mai Rut was Chinese; the people there had an accent. When we arrived, they already had a house divided into rooms for us to sleep in. Other camps had loudspeakers that announced the curfew, but Mai Rut had no curfew. Every Saturday or Sunday, they would let us out of the camp to go to the beach, about a 45-minute walk away. My uncle would buy pineapple or watermelon. We would strip it down and sell it. They would let us do that. I think that was the most fun place.

At that camp the INS prepared us to come to the United States. They took the whole family's picture with us in front of the blackboard. Then they tested us with a translator. "Why do you want to go to the USA?" they asked. They asked my uncle what he did for a living before the Khmer Rouge. He told them he was a soldier, which was true. As a soldier he would only come home two times a year because he had to go to training. He also owned a mining company.

After five months at Mai Rut, our next stop was the Philippines. I don't remember how we got there. It must have been by plane. From the capital city we took a bus to the camp. That was the best camp. A stream, a forest; it was beautiful. Everybody wanted to stay there. You could eat everything over there. The Philippine people loved the Cambodians. They didn't like the Vietnamese; they thought they were stealing their cows for food.

Everybody had to go to school. Even my uncle couldn't stop me. You had to, or you could not go to the United States. In school they showed us the United States on TV. I was not afraid. I knew my life there would be better than this.

We had to learn English in the morning. They called it ESL and ESO. I don't know what ESO means. I didn't make friends in the ESL class. They already knew English and I didn't. They put me down. Their moms and dads must have been rich or something. They knew books one and two and there I was: A-B-C, 1-2-3. They put me in the same class and I looked like an idiot. I went to school shaking all the time.

But after school I had fun. I went to the stream, and crossed the stream to gather wood. I went to the beach. If you had money you could go by bicycle-taxi, but I walked. It took about three hours, but it was fun.

A lot of neighbors there were nice to me because they knew I was not my uncle's daughter. They could hear the yelling and screaming coming from my uncle's house. It was really his wife who made things hard. I called her Auntie, but she didn't treat me the same as her own kids. I don't blame her because she had a lot to deal with. But she never got me a bra or underwear. When I could make my own money in the United States I finally bought a bra and underwear. It was unbelievable.

We had to check twice a week at the INS to see if our name came up. If you missed it, you could lose your sponsor. Finally, in January of 1982, we came to the United States. When we left the camp, I saw all these people crying because they wouldn't see each other anymore, but I had no friends so I didn't cry. The new bus smell was awful and I got more bus sick than anyone in the family. For six hours I slept, threw up, slept and threw up. My aunt thought I was doing it to get attention! We left the next morning on a plane.

On the day we went to the airport, each family had to take off their clothes and turn around. They were checking for chicken pox or something, I don't know. It was the first time I learned that other women had pubic hair. I thought I was the only one and was afraid and thought maybe I should shave it. But during the inspections I saw that my aunt had it too and then I knew all women had pubic hair.

There were only two Cambodian families on the plane. The other family was going to Minnesota, too. They didn't speak a word of English, and I still didn't know English. No one on the plane spoke Khmer. So when the flight attendant asked me what I wanted to drink, I just said what the guy next to me said, "Beer!"

The lady shook her head. My uncle said, "No!" He knew what beer was. Then, when she asked me what I wanted to eat, I saw what someone else had and I just pointed to it.

We made a lot of stops: Singapore, Tokyo. I thought Tokyo was part of the United States. I went around the nice stores, trying on perfume and smelling all over the place. They must have thought I was crazy, but they didn't mind. I'd look around and say: I will look like this. The place I will live will look like this. It was all so pretty. The next stop was San Francisco. That's where they gave us coats, snow jackets, gloves and boots. All of us put them on right away. Everyone in San Francisco had on short skirts and here we were wearing boots, gloves and hats. But it was cold for us. In San Francisco, we still slept in the day and woke up at night to eat. It took about two months for us to adjust to the time change.

They provided us a house until we found our sponsor. Every time my uncle went to the toilet he'd put his two feet on the seat and squat, and I thought, why don't you just sit? When we used the water, we took a container and filled one with hot water and the other with cold. We did this for two weeks. Then our English teacher came and asked how we took showers. When we showed her, she said, no, and told us how to mix the water. She also showed us how to use the stove. I only needed to be shown once and I knew how to do things.

That was when I had my first period, when I was sixteen and a half. In Cambodia, you have it late, sometimes at eighteen. I didn't know what a period was. I was walking around the house and I started dripping. In Cambodia, in the water, there are leeches, but I knew there were no leeches here. My uncle's wife wasn't there at first but when she came home I asked her what was wrong with me. She said I was grown up now. In Cambodia we call it *kromom*. You cannot have sex before you have your period. Now I knew it was okay for me to marry.

We could not find a tampon so she showed me how to take toilet paper and fold it, and fold it, then change it when it got too wet. I used a whole roll in one day because I didn't know anything. My period lasted two weeks. Then my aunt's daughter had it too.

We were still waiting for a sponsor. When we got one, my uncle said our destination was Florida. Then all of a sudden the Florida sponsor didn't want us anymore, I guess. So we stayed there another three months, but it was nice. The people living downstairs, who worked for the government, made enough for us to eat and gave us food.

Finally we got a sponsor in Minnesota. Her name was Mary. She was Sopheap Yin's sponsor, too. She had prepared a house for us, already. For the first month she bought us food, everything. She made sure we had everything in the house we needed, and provided clothes for us to wear. She took us shopping for clothes, until we got used to doing it ourselves.

In Minnesota we prayed at a small temple. The old people were very nice there, and it seemed like we were all together.

But there was still a lot to get used to. I always stared at people who were kissing. I said, "Why are they doing that? What's that for?" In Cambodia no one hugs, no one shakes hands and no one kisses. We greet each other by putting our hands together and bowing. Very respectful and polite.

I thought snow would be big pieces of ice falling from the sky. I thought it would be more like hail because we had hail in Cambodia. When I first saw it, I wanted to eat it all. I took a whole bunch of snow, made a ball and poured syrup in the middle. I ate so much I got diarrhea.

But the problem was that my uncle and his wife kept moving because there was a limit to Welfare and my uncle had to find jobs. For almost five months of ninth grade, I went to John Marshall High School in Rochester, Minnesota, and I made some friends. But then my uncle moved to St. Cloud where I went to Apollo High School for not even a year. I just started to make some friends there, and we moved again, to Wisconsin. That's where I finished high school.

In the locker room at school I covered my eyes so I wouldn't see the other naked girls. There were three Cambodians in the school, each of us in a different swimming class, but the teacher thought we were all the same person. All of us cried in swimming class because we didn't like wearing bathing suits. We were too modest. The teacher let us wear long T-shirts over them. Usually people would use two towels to cover themselves, but I'd use five.

My uncle stayed in Wisconsin about three months and then decided to move to California. In California you had to finish high school when you were eighteen, but if I was going to finish, I knew I'd have to be older than that. So that's when I said I'd had enough. I don't even know why I wanted to finish high school so much. But I didn't go with them.

First, I stayed with this lady, but then she moved to Minnesota and said I had to find my own place to live. I didn't know where to go, so I went to Social Services. By then I knew a little English. I sat there on a chair in a hallway from nine in the morning until they were closing. The woman who worked there asked me, "What are you doing here, honey?"

I said, "I don't know where to go. I have no place to live."

And I sat there and she said, "What happened to you mom and dad?"

I said, "I don't want to move with my uncle to California."

"So he is not your real dad?"

I explained that for me to come to the United States my uncle and his wife had to say I was their daughter.

She and some other people there made phone calls everywhere. Finally they found a place for me in a group home for kids who wouldn't listen to their mom and dad, who had problems. I had to stay there for five or six months until they could find me a foster family.

The kids there picked on me. They were not nice, except for one girl, Julie. I've tried to find her and I can't. Her mom was Japanese and her dad was American, and had been a general in the Second World War; that's how her parents met. Julie had problems with her father because he was not fair to her mom. Her mom had cancer, and Julie would fight with her father because he would not take care of her mother. He was not a nice man.

Anyway, every time the other girls gave me a hard time, Julie would stand up for me. I didn't have money to buy clothes and Julie worked in the Montgomery Ward store, so when she bought something for herself she got something for me, too. We were the same size. She was very nice, a very sweet girl.

I never regretted not going to California with my uncle's family. In 1993 my uncle went to visit Cambodia and never came home. Then his wife died. None of the kids finished high school. One of them is in jail. One son, Jonathan, is retarded. Three are married. I feel so awful for the kids because I know what it's like not to have a mom and a dad. I keep in touch with them because they are part of my family. The kids are nice to me, now. Then, they were mean to me. They would say I was not their real sister. But I forgive them. They were just kids.

Just before I turned eighteen I moved in with my foster family. They were really nice. The man's name was Mr. Chuck Hanson. His wife helped the community as a volunteer. They had two sons, Eric and Matthew. They were sweet boys. Eric was eight and Matthew was close to seven. Mr. Hanson's mom had had ten kids. It was amazing. They were very well-educated people and very religious. Every year my foster mom sends me pictures of Matthew and Eric. Matthew wants to become a pilot. Eric graduated from Boston University. My foster mom called to tell me Eric is now engaged to a girl from Russia. They met each other at Boston University. The family still lives in Wisconsin. I lived with them for less than a year. When I turned eighteen, I moved out.

I lived with Rada Chhan, a friend from high school. It seemed like I was repeating grades all the time, but it was because of the moves and the language. Rada was like a sister to me, and her mom was very nice. Every time we came home from school, she always prepared food for us. One bowl for Rada, one bowl for me, one for Rada's younger sister and another for her brother. She was a very sweet lady and I considered her to be like my mom. I slept next to her all the time. Her daughters didn't sleep with her, but I did. I needed to, because I missed my mom. I had missed her a lot, and I'd also been an only child. I never had time to speak to my mother, to hug her, to kiss her. We were always separated.

My mom was tiny. She was half-Vietnamese and half-Cambodian. She was light-skinned. She was sweet to me, but it's hard to remember when you don't live with someone that long.

I graduated in 1987, and Rada graduated in 1988. Rada had to move down to Minnesota one year before I graduated because she was reaching the age-cut for help from Social Services and Welfare in Wisconsin. I stayed with a friend of mine for four or five months. Then I moved down with Rada again. She got married before we both finished high school. She lived with her husband, her mom, me, one of her brothers and two sisters. Then Rada moved to Lawrence, and in 1988 I moved to Lawrence, too, and lived with Rada and her husband. They'd told me there were a lot of job openings there.

Way back in 1985, there was a band playing in a basement, and that's when my husband said he saw me for the first time. He was sitting on the stairway. He said he remembered my words, "If you sit on the stairs, I'm going to step on you." Stomp! I didn't even know it was him. He was in my way. He said he'd seen me a lot of times; I never saw him, not until I lived with him at Rada's place. Rada stayed home and prepared food, and Voeun would pay her two hundred dollars a month. His name is Voeun Toeur. He came to the US a year after me. He had two brothers and one sister. His mom had a really hard life. The Khmer Rouge took her husband away and put him in a prison camp in1977. Heuk, Rada's husband, and my husband are cousins. They carry the same last name.

My husband worked for Columbo Yogurt and after I moved in 1989, he started getting sick a lot. His brother said, "I've never seen you sick before. Why are you sick now?" He'd stay home with me and Rada and he'd play card games with us, for fun. He'd never played cards before.

I don't know why, but I never trusted guys. I wanted to be far away from guys. But I trusted him. It seemed OK. He was all right. I was comfortable with him.

I had never been with a guy before and I knew nothing about birth control. I'd taken Health in high school, but maybe it was just me not knowing enough English. The first time I had sex, I had a baby. I knew I was pregnant in April. I was twenty-four at that time, and my husband was four years older. I had Kelly, my first son, December 16.

I was happy. I never regretted it. My husband walked me through the rough spots. I needed a car, transportation to go to work. Rada loaned me money to get a car. My husband helped me with insurance and made my car payments. The car cost over $10,000! That was real nice of him. More than I expected. I had never been with a person as nice as that. This was the first time.

I worked the third shift at a fiberglass company in Haverhill, making nylon. Oh, it was itchy. I couldn't stand it. I didn't want to work there, but I was too afraid to say I wanted to quit. So I stopped going. They fired me and I wasn't sad at all, I was happy. It was just so itchy. All the clothes that I wore there I had to throw away.

We were real close and we moved in together. My husband took care of me. Even when I couldn't go to work, he bought me food and paid rent. I've been very lucky. My husband is very watchful with money. In two years he saved ten thousand dollars. He's not like me. I want something and I've got to get it. I can't say no. If he has a twenty-dollar bill he won't break it. I will.

My husband wouldn't let me go back to work until Kelly was almost a year old. Then I worked at Champion Foil, a factory in Newburyport. I worked there from 1991 to 1996. But then my husband's mother had a stroke. She could not blink one eye and she could not take care of my third son, Kody, anymore. She would carry Kody, and he would start to fall out of her arms. My husband was so scared. He worked the second shift and he didn't get enough sleep at all. He went in at midnight and came home at five in the morning. It was awful.

Since 1996, I've worked at a lot of places and I've been self-employed. I made necklaces and worked with computers for almost one year. Then got laid off. Then I began working for the Asian Center. I've thought about going back to school but every time I read something, I get a headache. But I bet if I went to school now it would be easier than when I first started, because I understand the language. I'm going to wait until Kody is in the sixth grade. It would be helpful, too, if I knew how to read and write Cambodian well.

My husband said he only wanted one kid. He wanted me to get my tubes tied after I had Kelly, but I didn't say anything to him. For me, because I'm so lonely, I always wanted two or three. It took four years for me to have Korry. I was so scared that I would just have one. I thought, oh my God, what if something happens to Kelly, my first son? I was so scared that I would have no more kids.

I thought Korry, my second child, would be a girl. But I had another boy, so I thought maybe I would follow in the footsteps of my mother-in-law. She had my husband, his younger brother, and then a girl. Maybe I'll be like her. But no, Kody came. And Kody is more than a handful. But when they all go to school, I feel lonely.

My husband and I have never been legally married. In Cambodia, after people get married they break up so fast. I want it to stay like this. If you break up you have to go to court later. So I've never been legally married.

Korry asks, "Why don't you get married, mommy?"

"Why, Korry?"

"You don't love my dad?"

"No, it's not that," I say. "Marriage doesn't matter. As long as you love each other and trust each other. That's all that counts."

Seeds of Lotus: Cambodian and Vietnamese Voices in America

Means of Escape

Translated by Hue Nguyen and Sister Le-Hang Le

Seeds of Lotus: Cambodian and Vietnamese Voices in America

To the future generations

of

Vietnamese-Americans

Seeds of Lotus: Cambodian and Vietnamese Voices in America

Introduction

Everyone was busy. They worked long hours, came home to cook for families, had grandchildren to watch and evening English classes to attend. To contribute six Thursday evenings to the making of this book was a lot to ask. Some contributors came, told their stories and did not return. Some wrote their stories in English. Some preferred to tell their stories to me in their own homes. And so the class began discouragingly disparate and unconnected.

But Hue Nguyen and I showed up each Thursday anyway, hoping someone would join us ready to speak, along with a few others who might be willing to listen. And there always was. And then those who'd come and gone came back, heard someone else's story, came again and stayed.

Slowly, the participants transcended generational differences, gained perspective on their immediate and individual concerns, and grew more committed to the goal of the project and to each other. And by the class's end there existed a connection and sense of community where five weeks before there'd been none.

So storytelling had worked its charm. What had happened within the microcosm of our class illustrated the very reason for its existence and for the existence of this book: to bring human beings together by sharing stories of what it is to be one.

Seeds of Lotus: Cambodian and Vietnamese Voices in America

Hung Van

Born 1923

Translated by Hue Nguyen

My wife heard about me from the matchmaker, but she never saw what I looked like and I never saw what she looked like until our wedding day. At that time in China, the man could see a picture of the woman only if she was a widow. And if a man left for Vietnam and didn't send for his wife within three years, then the wife could marry someone else.

I came to Vietnam in 1947, a year and a half before my wife, when I was about twenty-four years old. I came for two reasons: to look for a job and because of Communism in China. That means I ran away twice: from China to Vietnam and from Vietnam to America.

In Vietnam, I started a small business that I ran for many years, selling fabric at the Vinh Long Mall. I made enough to feed my ten children, and because I had so many children, I did not have to join the army.

Then in 1968, on Vietnamese New Year, my store was burned down. My house was near the market, so I could see the fire. The Viet Cong were in our city a couple of blocks away, stationed in the local cinema. They were fighting with the South Vietnamese soldiers and we were afraid that they were heading toward our neighborhood. So we left, followed the river into the countryside and sought refuge in a church because we figured that the soldiers of both sides would respect a church building and not harm us. As we were moving along, we saw a V.C. soldier get shot and killed while he was shooting at a helicopter.

By then we were too scared to continue on and a man we met on the way offered us shelter in his brick house. He let us in, showed us where he kept the food, and then he continued on to the church.

When the shooting and bombing finally stopped three or four days later, we returned to our house. We heard from the one family that had stayed behind that the Viet Cong shot up at a helicopter, and the helicopter had shot back at a house. Then they left. The Viet Cong left too, but the house had caught on fire, and the family saved the house from burning down. So when we returned, we were relieved to see that our house and neighborhood were still there.

Because my store had been destroyed, I opened a bakery. I would bake the goods at my house, then put them in a box on the front of a big tricycle, and ride to the Vinh Long Mall to deliver them to stores wholesale. I did this until 1975 when the Communists took over and forbade me to continue my business.

The Communists ordered all of us to change our money into the North and South general money and everyone's share had to be equal, about five hundred dollars, which was not enough money to invest in my business and not enough money for anyone to be able to buy baked goods, anyway. The government limited all our food, allowing us only ten pounds of rice a week and a little bit of pork. And government officials scared us by often showing up at our door unannounced, just to check on us, carrying guns and accompanied by the village leaders.

In Vinh Long I lived in a two-story brick house. The first floor had been for my bakery business, and we used the second floor to sleep. The government said the house was nice and big and that they could use it for their offices. We wrote a letter, showed them a blueprint and papers that proved we'd paid our taxes and were the legal owners, but the government took it anyway without giving me any money in return. They simply gave us a smaller house to live in. That's when I began to think of leaving.

We decided that our two middle children should escape first— Mui, my daughter who was twenty-three, and my son, Chanh, who was fifteen. They knew how to speak and write both Chinese and Vietnamese, so when they reached a refugee camp they'd be able to write to both our Vietnamese and our Chinese relatives who'd already immigrated to other parts of the world. The rest of us would leave when Mui and Chanh reached America and had made enough money to sponsor and support us. In the meantime, I bought land and I grew papaya, guava, water apples, bananas and rice. My wife had learned to farm when she'd lived in China. It was hard, but I had to do it to survive. We ate some of what I grew, and I paid a government tax.

After Mui and Chanh left, I couldn't sleep for a month, not until I received news from them. And then finally a letter arrived from Mui, telling us that they had arrived safely and were in Thailand at a refugee camp. My wife and I and three of our unmarried children joined them in America on the first of October 1991, ten years later.

Mui Van

Born 1957

Translated by Hue Nguyen

My brother and I began our escape around eleven p.m. on a July night in 1980. I was twenty-three and he was fifteen. My cousins came to my house, quickly woke us up and told us it was time to go. My nephew woke up too. He was only six and he said, "Where are you going?" I said, "I have to go to the capital, but don't say anything to anyone." He wanted to go with me, but I said no. Later, he also escaped, but we never heard from him again, and so he must have died. I still feel bad that I didn't take him with me that night.

We only took with us two pairs of clothes and walked in the direction of my uncle's house on a quiet street under yellow streetlights. My uncle's house was very big, surrounded by an acre of land and near a river. His backyard was also near the house of one of the Communist city leaders and when I heard a dog's bark coming from that direction, I was frightened. We had to take a different route, a roundabout route from my uncle's house to my cousin's boat, and I didn't know the way. It was very dark. There was no moon. But we had someone to lead us.

The boat was docked beside my uncle's land. It was sixteen by three meters, and it had a motor on the back. My cousins had put a lot of palm leaves in it so that it would look like we were going to sell them, but really they were for us to hide beneath. Once we were out on the river, we filled empty twenty liter bottles with the river water for drinking.

Out on the open sea, we threw all the leaves into the water, and that's when the police spotted us. They chased and shot at us, but the boat was fast enough to get away. The boat had a good captain who used the stars to navigate. We also had a compass onboard, and it helped once we'd outrun the police, and the pilot and a military man had to figure out which way we had to go; but the compass didn't help when we hit a storm.

Luckily, we met up with a British naval ship and about three people from our boat climbed up and asked them to help us through the storm. So they tied our boat to theirs which helped protect us from the wind, but they didn't give us any food, and the next morning when the storm was over, they just cut the rope and let us go adrift. We also discovered that our rudder was broken, but the boat crew fixed it. Even so, we were lost on the sea for about seven days.

There were twenty-six people in the boat, mostly my relatives, but also a few outsiders, people who spoke English. I spent most of the time lying down under a kind of roof. It was dark, and I was sick the whole time. I didn't go to the bathroom for seven days. My cousin had given me some ginseng to put in my mouth which curbed my hunger and thirst, and I was too seasick to be afraid.

The couple next to me had just gotten married. They had a lot of jewelry and food with them, but nobody wanted to steal anything from anyone. We were all too tired and sick. Eventually, though, the couple did get robbed.

Just before we landed, Thai pirates pulled two boats up on either side of ours and then jumped in. They grabbed a girl to take onto their boat, and her brother-in-law pretended to be her husband and begged them to let her stay, because sometimes they left married women alone. But they ignored him and took her anyway. His real wife, her sister, was holding their baby, so they didn't take her.

I didn't know they were there until they came to get me. Just in case this happened, I'd been told to wear some jewelry so I quickly gave one of them my earrings and he went away. But two others came down and threatened me with knives and hammers and told me to come with them, but before I was even up on deck, I heard noises and looked over at their boat to see a woman lying down, and I knew something terrible was going on, so I ran away from them, back and forth on my boat. I wanted to die rather than be kidnapped by them, so I asked a man on my boat, "How can I die? How can I die?" I had nothing to kill myself with. The pirates continued chasing me with knives and hammers, so I grabbed the man's daughter, and the man said I was his wife. They didn't listen to him and ordered me up onto the roof of my boat to take me into theirs. One of them reached down for my hand, but I didn't want to touch him. I jumped up on the roof myself and then collapsed there like I was dead. One of my cousins said, "She must be dead," and the pirates stood around me for a moment and then left me alone. I opened my eyes a little and saw that they'd pulled their second boat up to the other side of ours, and I saw my brother in it and thought, he's only a teenager, he's too young. I can't die. I have to take care of him.

The pirates came back and ordered me into the same boat as my brother. I saw the little girl there again, so I held her tight, protecting us both while the pirates on our boat pulled out our clothes and ripped the seams looking for hidden jewelry. My mother had sewn my grandmother's gold ring and a gold chain into the seams of the pants I wore, so they never found them. What they didn't steal, they threw into the ocean.

When they let us back onto our boat I remember seeing a girl with no clothes on. A man threw a pair of pants to her so she could cover herself. Only a long time afterward, when we were in America, did she tell me that she had been raped.

In the afternoon of the same day, we saw an oil rig. Three people from our boat who spoke Chinese, English, and Vietnamese boarded it to ask them for directions to land. They gave us directions to Thailand along with ten barrels of gasoline, and we continued on our way.

Later that night, a fourteen or fifteen-year-old boy suddenly staggered inside and fell right on top of me. His head was bleeding and I didn't know what was going on, but then I realized that we were under attack again by more Thai or Malaysian pirates. They'd thrown something at the boy from their boat, like a piece of iron, then they boarded our boat, robbed us of all our gasoline and tried to sink us by making a hole in the bottom. But luckily my brother saw it and quickly plugged it up with some clothing. Still, the boat filled with a lot of water, and we all had to bail it out with pots and pans and anything else we could find.

The next morning I heard someone say they saw land, and when I looked up I saw coconut trees and a beach, people and boats. Everyone in our boat was quiet, scared we'd be attacked by more pirates. The boat owner saw some soldiers on shore, so he got out and asked them for help. They didn't understand Vietnamese and he didn't understand their language, but soon it was clear they didn't want us there because a Malaysian naval ship threw us a rope and towed us back out to sea. We were afraid our boat was going to break into pieces. Everyone was crying and shouting, but I just sat there quietly. After a couple of hours they left us there.

Then we saw a fishing boat. Again, we were afraid that they were Thai pirates, but they waved at us, and as we came closer we heard them calling to us in Vietnamese, and that was when we knew we were safe. My brother and cousins recognized the crew. They were friends of ours. We lived in the same district. They had already escaped and were living in a Thai refugee camp. Since the Thai were in control, they made people in the camp fish for them and paid them by giving them some of the catch.

We followed the fishing boat to shore, and a Vietnamese man in the boat got out and helped us walk from our boat onto land because we were so weak, staggering and swaying back and forth. All I had to take with me was one pair of clothes.

The whole time on the boat, I hadn't thought about home, nor had I felt sorry that I had left Vietnam. I just wanted to get to the camp and run away.

Someone ran to the camp to tell the officials that we were there while we waited on the beach. There were a lot of coconut trees on shore and a fish sauce house with a tin roof. It looked like a bus station and was surrounded by a wooden fence. We slept outside of it, under the porch. The village used it as a small temporary camp.

The next day, the Red Cross arrived and gave us big white plastic bags with a red cross on the outside of them filled with towels and soap and clothes. Then we all went to a small hospital where we received check-ups and were given medicine for any infections. They also said if you write a letter quickly, we will send it for you. I wrote to my parents. I told them that we had been on the boat for nine days and that we were safe. But I couldn't tell them anymore than that because we had to write it fast, and the people from the Red Cross were waiting for us to finish.

On the second day I found out that I was on the border of Thailand and Malaysia and I exchanged my ring for Thai money. The ring had belonged to my grandmother. She told me, "When I die, I'm going to give you this ring." But when I knew I was going to leave Vietnam, I knew I would need it sooner than that. I asked her if she would make a trade. "I'll give you my ring for yours," I said. Of course her ring was much more valuable, but she agreed.

The women and children stayed in the camp while the men went out to trade and sell things, so I gave the ring to my cousin-in-law, Ty, who owned the boat. I never saw who bought the ring and I wasn't sad about it. I needed the money for food.

We lived at the Maruad camp for twenty days, then we were transferred to Songkhla Camp in Thailand. I traveled there for half a day by bus and was glad to leave.

Outside Songkhla, we saw a big gate and a high barbed wire fence, but the camp itself was right on a white, sandy beach lined with pine trees and was beautiful.

Vietnamese soldiers who had escaped first, had worked for the UNHCR (United Nations High Commission for Refugees) and built the camp for the people who came after. They built barracks with palm leaf roofs and wooden platforms for floors. There were no walls, and it was the roof supports that divided twenty families that lived in each. At night, we covered ourselves with mosquito nets.

In the very early morning, I would get up and exercise by taking a swim in the sea. Then I would go to school to learn English. After

I had been there only two days, a young guy told me he was leaving and sold me and my cousins his hand blender and glasses, table and chairs, so that I could earn a living making and selling soybean milk. I bought the soybeans at the market outside the camp which was open each day from nine to eleven. Then I soaked them, cooked them and made them into the milk that I sold by the glass. To buy the drink, my customers used money that had been sent to them by relatives who'd already immigrated to other countries. I sold the milk for a month, but I made no profit and it took up all my time.

Then, one day I found out that my neighbor was transferring to another camp. He asked me what language I spoke and what my nationality was. I told him I was Chinese and that I spoke Mandarin dialect. The neighbor introduced me to a Thai woman who worked at the market selling luggage and medicine. He had been her interpreter and thought I could replace him. So that became my new job. My brother also worked for another merchant at the market, as a translator in the Chau Chou dialect. This job gave me more time. I only spent two hours in the morning interpreting and then I could study English all afternoon.

I also needed time to write a lot of letters to relatives in Australia, Canada and America. A cousin in Australia sent us money and another cousin in America sponsored me to come to Lawrence, Massachusetts. He had come to America in 1979.

After I was at Songkhla for three months, I was transferred to a camp in Indonesia called Galang. There, I would climb to the top of the mountain to observe at the Buddhist temple and from up there the camp looked like a big birdcage. The barracks had orange roofs and were more like real houses. I saw people bathing and washing clothes. It was a beautiful picture.

At Galang, we slept in bunk beds. They gave us rice, canned food to eat, dried vegetables in bags and some beans I sprouted. I also planted a little patch of vegetables so I could eat some fresh food. We had very little water. We had to walk up a hill where they supplied us with about three gallons of water, one for each person each day to use for cooking and personal hygiene. The water I could have used to wash my face and teeth, I used instead to grow the vegetables.

People kept asking me to combine my money with theirs so we could open a small business, but in Galang, one member of each family had to know English to be accepted by the Delegation. I decided not to go into any business because I wanted to be sure I had time to go to school to learn English.

In the morning I walked a half mile to go to school for art class and to learn tailoring for job training. I learned English in the afternoon. In the evening, I studied and on the weekends we were free and I walked an hour to the beach with my school friends. We would have picnics on the beach and when the tide went down we'd go swimming.

I stayed there four months and then I had an interview with the U.S. Delegation. One person interviewed me, but there were other people sitting at the table. After my interview, I learned about life in America like how to shop. From there, I was transferred to Singapore for three days and there I didn't need to cook. They gave us food, and we just had to wait to leave. So all I had to do was go to the mall.

In 1981, I left with my brother and three cousins for America. At first we lived for about twenty days in a shelter and my first teacher in the U.S., named Judy, came to teach us English. After that, my three cousins, brother and I rented an apartment and two other teachers, named Carol and Bob, helped us.

My younger brother went to Lawrence High School. After school he went directly to work in a restaurant. He'd come home tired and want to see his friends, but I always said no, because he had to rest and do his homework. On the weekends he could see his friends. He is successful. He studied electronic engineering at Northeastern, but now he works in computer software engineering.

I had to go to school too, to continue to study English at Northern Essex Community College and to become a citizen. And because I also had to have money to put in the bank. I worked part-time at a newspaper company and at a restaurant. Two years later I married. When I had my first child I stopped going to school and stayed home. After my second child was born, I went back to work full-time at the Gillette company. I didn't have money for a babysitter, so I worked the night shift in factories and stayed home during the day to care for my children. I worked a lot: full-time, over-time. It was very hard, but my husband and I needed money to buy a house and to sponsor my parents, my sister and my other younger brother; and my husband had eight people in his family to sponsor. We saved enough to sponsor them, but not to buy a house. After my third child was born, I went back to school to get an Associates Degree in Computer Science and Commercial Art Desktop Publishing. My parents arrived here in 1991, four months after my in-laws. That was when I finished my degree, but I continued to work factory jobs for the convenience of the hours.

Even after everyone arrived, I still had worries and responsibilities. I sent my brothers, sisters, brother and sister-in-law and my parents to school to learn English. I wanted them to have something to do and to keep them from feeling lonely. My husband and I sent my younger brother and sister to high school, along with my husband's six siblings.

You can have a lot of dreams about coming here, but you also have to know how to take care of yourself and others. To do it you have to have a strong mind, strong heart and your health. I was responsible for a lot of people. If I didn't take care of them, they would not have a good future. So life in America has been very busy and I'm grateful to everyone who helped me get here. Now, the only thing I'd like for myself would be a little free time.

T. Nguyen

Born 1933

Translated by Le-Hang Le

I lived in my grandfather's house with my aunt and uncle, mother and father. Before 1945 my grandfather was the richest person in our village in the Son Tay Province. He ran a wine bar and bought French wine from merchants in Hanoi, then transported it to the countryside to sell it in his store. My aunt and uncle took over the business. They sold the wine by the glass to French military personnel, pouring it from bottles lined up on the wall behind them. Our house was made of brick. It had a refrigerator that was full of meat and wine and beer. But after 1945 we began to suffer.

My uncle, my aunt's brother, was a member of the Quoc Dan Dang Party. He was also rich. The Communists hated that party and hated the rich. They killed some of my cousins and they sentenced my uncle to death. While he was awaiting execution, he committed suicide. He would have disemboweled himself, but because he had no knife, he cut his wrists with the glass from the face of his watch, and as he did so, he said to the guards, "Come here and look at my liver. I will show my liver to you." The liver, in Vietnam, represents a person's strength and courage.

When I was three years old, my father died, and my mother continued to live with my father's side of the family until she remarried. When she left the household to live with her new husband, she wanted to take my younger sister and me, her only son. But when a woman remarries in Vietnam, she is scorned. So my aunt, my father's sister, forbade her to take us. She beat my mother, and I remember my mother was bleeding from the nose and the mouth. She had to give in. She did not want to leave us, but my father's family had all the power, and she could not bear it. It made me very sad.

My mother lived about five kilometers away, which at the time was very far. I didn't visit her, but she came to visit me. I also saw my stepfather, who was a kind man. But then I left for Hanoi in 1954 and I didn't see her again until 1976 when I was living in Saigon. A cousin of mine who lived in France told her where I was. She traveled down from Hanoi to see me, and when we met again, the love was still there, but we were not close, not like when I was young.

My mother returned to Hanoi and she died in 2003 at the age of ninety. My aunt also died in 2003 when she was ninety-five years old. Both of them had suffered and had never had enough food to eat, but my family has genes for a long life.

Before my mother left, I had gone to school, so I'd learned how to read and write. But after she left, I stopped attending school and stayed home to help with my aunt's household. The uncle who committed suicide had owned the house. Like my father, my aunt's husband died of a simple illness that was fatal because of lack of medicine. So she was a widow. Also, part of my household was my younger sister, my aunt's son, my aunt's sister, her two children and her husband, who was Chinese. At that time, the Communists liked the Chinese so they left him alone.

My widowed aunt was not kind to me. She was not kind to her own son or to my younger sister and my two cousins. She was very strict and she beat all of us with a rod. Here, in America, you would call it abuse, but in Vietnam it's more acceptable.

Before 1945, life was free, like in America, but then, when I was twelve or thirteen, the Communists came into our village and on a loudspeaker ordered us to destroy our homes and all our property. So my aunt sold our house. She sold the roof, the windows, the doors, the chairs and so on. The people who bought everything lived further out in the countryside and didn't have such nice things. But the Communists just hadn't gotten to them yet. Eventually, they went into their villages and ordered them to destroy their houses, too.

The kitchen was separate from the main house, so we lived there for a while. Then we moved into the homes of other people, people who had houses made of palm leaves. So between 1945 and 1948 we suffered materially and spiritually, moving around the small villages outside of Hanoi. We never had enough rice to eat. Only vegetables and no meat. My aunt sold food from a cart. I helped by doing household work. Finally, in 1948 we had to escape from the villages and hide in the city of Hanoi. And in 1953 I joined the French army until I was discharged in 1955. With the army I moved down to Saigon.

In Saigon, I made a living by fixing bicycles and watches; an uncle had taught me how when I was fifteen. I also wanted to be a teacher. My father had died when I was young, and my mother had re-married and left me by myself, so I wanted to know many ways to support myself. At night I attended school. I began in 1955, graduated in 1960, and began teaching elementary school. Then I went back to school in 1971 to earn a certificate to teach high school. It's usually a two-year degree, but I completed it in one and began teaching high school math in 1973. Throughout the war, I lived and taught in Saigon. Most of the fighting was on the outskirts of the city, so in the center of the city it was pretty safe.

When the Communists took over in 1975 I stopped teaching. And for the next ten years I fixed bicycles and watches. All the teaching positions related to Communism, and I refused to work in a Communist system. Luckily, I was not sent to a re-education camp, but life was not good. The Communists did not change the curriculum for math, but my salary was not enough to support my family. I had three sons and one daughter. My wife had to start a small business as a vendor, selling cookies and cakes from a cart on the street. She made enough to buy us vegetables, but no meat. I was lucky that I had a cousin who had married a Frenchman, and so had left the country early. She sent money to us from where she lived in Nice, France. In 1985, the situation improved in Vietnam, so I went back to teaching school and retired in 1993.

Many had a dream to go to the West and I was one of them, but I could not afford it, so I sent my second son who was only fifteen years old. I knew he was quick in math and science, better than my oldest son, Nhan, who is a very religious Buddhist and not very materialistic, and I knew America was famous for its technology. I figured my second son, Van, had a good chance of being successful there. Before he left, I told him to go to no other country but America.

I paid $1,000 for him to escape by boat. I waited for two weeks and then I heard that Van was in Paulo Bidong in Malaysia. Because he was a minor, he was already in America by the end of 1986. My cousin, my aunt's only son, was living in Reading, Massachusetts, and I had another cousin living in California.

I lived with my first son for thirty-three years in Vietnam. Now I live with my second son and my daughter-in-law in Tewksbury, Massachusetts. And my biggest problem is my wife's unhappiness. She stays home to take care of our two granddaughters and cooks for the whole family. She goes to school to learn English, but can't remember any vocabulary. But the worst problem is that she and my daughter-in-law do not get along. My daughter-in-law belittles her, says she doesn't know anything, that she's ignorant. She doesn't speak respectfully to her.

My daughter-in-law came to the U.S. in 1992 and works full-time as an assembly-line supervisor. The conflict between my wife and daughter-in-law makes my wife cry, and she says if it weren't for me, she'd go back to Vietnam. She misses our other children who still live there. I have no problem with our daughter-in-law; but I can't solve the problem between the two of them. Many Vietnamese women who come here have similar difficulties. They are upset with their children in America and want to go back.

A friend once told me that in America, ladies are always first, and if you don't know how to live in their family, the wife will kick you out. In the Vietnamese community there's a joke about it: ladies first, dog second, children third, car fourth, house fifth, man sixth, parents tenth.

Chon Thi Lo

Born 1951

Written by Chon Thi Lo

In 1980, my husband left Vietnam to come to America. We knew then that it was a dangerous, potentially fatal journey, so we decided that he should leave first without me and our son, Danh, to pave the way for us to follow. After his departure, I attempted to escape Vietnam twice, and it was only luck that my son and I were not captured and thrown into jail.

My husband, however, was successful, and afterward at night, government officials would knock on our door and check to see if I had any strangers visiting, but with the ulterior motive of checking on my activities. They'd come in the house and peer into the rooms and closets with flashlights. Most of the time, they did not give any reason at all. I never told them anything. Sometimes they called me to their office and asked me questions about my husband, the reason behind his disappearance. I told them that he did not love us and had left without a word. Because of these incidents, my father-in-law and sixteen-year-old sister-in-law, Út, stayed with us, afraid for our safety.

No one had phones and you had to pay to receive letters that the government opened and censored anyway, but I heard from my husband three days after he left. The people who'd taken him had returned with a letter from him saying he'd arrived safely. They gave it to my friend, who then gave it to me. After that, I tried to live a normal life. I ran a grocery store with Út out of the first floor of my house and took care of Danh, who, at the time, was three and half years old. After work, I would take Danh out to eat, bring him to a park, and then bring him back home. On one particular day, my cousin came to visit. He told me that his neighbor's sister owned a business that took people across the borders of Cambodia and Thailand. She charged ten ounces of gold for an adult and two ounces for children under ten. I decided it was a small price to pay for freedom.

My cousin told me to cut my hair, darken my skin and learn to speak Khmer to help hide my Vietnamese identity and so increase my chances of escape. My hair was down to my waist and at a beauty salon I had it cut above my shoulders. Everyone was surprised and wondered why I'd done it. I packed old clothes, dried cakes made of sweet rice and mung beans and limes dried with sugar that we could suck on, foods I'd been told that were good for the kind of journey we were taking, and I packed enough to last for five to seven days. I asked one of my other cousins to open the soles of Danh's sandals, hide some gold inside and glue them back together again. He did it with no questions asked. And I sewed my gold chains into my shirt collar.

The leader chose to leave during the New Year, because she knew that was when Thailand and Cambodia imposed fewer border restrictions on visiting family members and the transport of goods. I could tell no one of my plans, so when my cousin arrived at nine a.m., to take me to the leader, I asked my sister-in-law to go shopping for me. I stood in my house and looked around, thinking of how I would never see it again. I wanted to cry, but my mother-in-law would have seen me, and had she found out what I was planning to do, she would have tried to stop me. She loved Danh so much. So I told myself to be strong. Don't cry. Then my cousin, Danh and I boarded a xich lô, which is a bike-drawn carriage, and we pulled away.

I heard that only a few days later government officials came to my house, and realizing that I wasn't there, boarded it up and allowed no one, not even my parents, to enter it again.

When I first saw the lady who would guide me to Cambodia she was sitting in the boat that would take us from Tan Chau, my hometown, to the border of Cambodia. The moment I sat down, she wrapped my head with a red and black striped scarf, a Cambodian kramah, to make me look less suspicious. She was seven years younger than my mother and could speak both Cambodian and Vietnamese. She was friendly, greeted me with a smile, but only told me softly to sit down. And though I did not know her, I found out that she knew about me and my two unsuccessful escapes. But for most of the trip, we rarely spoke, and I simply sat there and watched the Mekong River pass beneath us.

At the border we took a xich lô to the house of the woman's relatives and at this point, I knew there was no turning back, not only because I was I determined to escape, but because turning back meant being caught and imprisoned or even worse.

At the house, while we waited for dark, the woman told me I'd be joined by four Vietnamese men along with a former government soldier who had recently been released from prison. Her sister, she said, and her nephew would be the ones to lead us to Thailand.

During dinner, everyone suddenly stopped eating to listen closely to the radio. The announcer was speaking Khmer, but from the looks on everyone's faces, I knew the news was not good. "What is it?" I asked. And the woman told me that because of the dangerous political situation in Vietnam, the Thailand-Cambodian border was closed indefinitely.

I could no longer eat or look at my son. "What am I going to do now?" I said to her. She said that I just had to wait, and while I waited I could work on learning the Cambodian culture and language, and I would have to dress in the traditional clothing like the sarong. So that's what I did. Every day, I sat or lay under the hot sun in order to tan my skin to make it resemble the darker Cambodian skin tone. And every morning, the woman brought me out to the market to buy food and help me practice Khmer. We also visited the capital city, Phnom Penh, and the King's palace which the Khmer Rouge had converted into torture chambers. The torture chambers were now piled to the ceiling with the skulls and bones of only a fraction of those they had killed, now displayed to commemorate the dead and as a reminder of the Khmer Rouge's brutal regime. It frightened me, but I prayed to the dead there for my escape. I also prayed at the local temple but I wondered if Buddha would understand Vietnamese so I tried saying my prayers to him in Khmer.

The woman who housed us was good to me. She accompanied me

everywhere I went. Even at night, she slept beside me, always on the floor because in Cambodia there were no tables, chairs or beds.

I spent a month like this, moving to three different houses to avoid suspicion, and then finally the good news came. They'd opened the borders. Once again, we planned a nighttime escape. The woman's sister and her twenty-one-year-old son met with us. The son was a soldier, and his army contacts would come in handy if we encountered any trouble.

Because a large group would draw too much attention, we separated into two. We intended to pass through the Thai border on business, and you can't bring children with you on business, so my son, Danh, joined the other four Vietnamese men and the soldier. But I wasn't far from him. While I walked, I could look up and see him tied to the back of a bicycle so he wouldn't fall off. I carried a handbag containing our clothes, towels and dried food, and as the sky darkened to black and we continued to walk, I grew tired and slowed my pace. Then the dirt road disappeared into the wild woods, and thorns pricked and scratched my legs and feet. Eventually, I dropped so far behind that I lost sight of my son.

There was no one around, just the forest on each side, and then suddenly, out of nowhere, I saw two Cambodian soldiers standing in front of us with guns on their shoulders. One of them was young, maybe eighteen or nineteen, and he said, "Stop. Are you Yun, Vietnamese? Or are you Cambodian?" I answered him in Khmer and then the leader tried talking to him too, but he only said, come with us, and led us to a camp in Nam Vang City in Cambodia. They ordered us into a tent and told us to lie down in a long row of cots, so they could loop one long chain around our ankles and around each of the beds. I looked around and saw that only my group had been caught, not Danh's, and I began to cry and ask for my son. Where was my son? But the woman leading us said that her son, the young soldier, had run away as soon as we'd seen the soldiers, and he was negotiating our release. We'd have to give her some of our gold to give to the soldiers. I ripped open my collar, gave her the gold chains, and it worked. In the morning, without a word, they took off the chain, and as I stepped out of the tent, there was my son, still tied on the bicycle. I ran up to him, cried and kissed him and said, "Thank God. I thought I'd lost you."

This time the soldier carried Danh on his back in a makeshift sling. But part of the deal he'd made for our release was that the other soldiers would give us a lift in their GMC. He warned us, though, not to speak to them, so I pretended we were mute. Even so, while we stood in the back of the truck with about twenty other soldiers, they talked a lot to Danh in Khmer, but I whispered to Danh not to say a word. That would not be easy for any three-year-old, but Danh understood and remained silent. That was, until they started eating some kind of snack that looked to us like big roaches. Then one of them turned around and threw one at Danh just to see if that would start him talking.

"Mom!" Danh said, "Those men eat roaches!" And so all the soldiers instantly knew that we were Vietnamese and said "Yun, Yun" over and over again. I thought this was it, that we were in real trouble now, but the truck just kept going, and the soldiers just continued to talk and eat and made no move to bring us back. A half hour later they let us off in the middle of the woods where we had to continue the journey by foot, and once again I was separated from my son.

The grass reached to my shoulders, and all I could see in every direction were trees. There was no clear path to follow. We stopped at a very poor looking thatched house to eat and to drink. There was no light, and because it was so dark inside, I could see people sleeping on the floor, but could not make out how many there were. Only an old lady was awake. We cooked some rice and ate it with dry salted fish, then drank some water and hurried to leave. While I walked, I heard the sound of gunshots and howling dogs and crickets. Snakes slithered under my feet. It was too dark to see far ahead, and I had no idea what time it was, but just kept walking in the dark and in the heat, and I became thirsty again, so I stopped at a small pond. It was very shallow and the water was dark green. I closed my eyes and drank from my palms and looked around for some wild fruit to eat, but saw only trees and grass.

The closer I got to Thailand, the hotter it became, and I wished for some rain to cool me off. The lady next to me helped carry my belongings, but I felt worse and worse. Finally, I just stopped in my tracks, certain I would die there from heat and exhaustion. But the leader and her son told me to keep going, that my son was coming and I had to keep going for him. Unlike me, my guide was as strong as ever, and I looked at her and began to walk again.

Just as we reached the border the sun rose. We approached an entry point and the soldiers there asked us why we'd come and where we intended to go in Thailand. I still was far from fluent in Khmer, so I was worried, but my guide took care of everything. She said that we were there on business intending to buy some goods to sell back in Cambodia. He let us pass, but I was so exhausted emotionally and physically I couldn't do much more than step over the line. The leader's son disappeared, and moments later returned with a bicycle so I could sit on it while he walked it to the place where we were to meet the other group and Danh.

Danh was already there. He was all wet with sweat and he ran up to me and said, "Mommy, where were you?" I said, "I'm here with you and we're okay. Everything's okay. Don't worry. Don't worry." Then I wrote my parents to tell them that Danh and I were all right and that we had reached a camp. A boy took two pictures of us. One was for me to keep and the other was for my parents. I paid him half the price and my parents would pay him the rest once they received the picture and saw my signature at the bottom.

I lived in crowded barracks without running water or toilets, and the camp guards took our money and jewelry. About three months after I had arrived, letters came from my family and my husband. It was the first news from him I'd received since the letter my friend had given to me three days after he'd left. It turned out that he'd been sponsored by an American family who had been against the Vietnam War. While he'd been establishing himself in American society, he had tried to contact us. Finally, he found us through the Red Cross in the refugee camp.

Six months after receiving his letter, Danh and I moved on to a second camp. There, we were allowed out to buy things that we needed, and we were given food that had already been prepared for us. We were given health checks and I filled out a lot of paperwork that enabled us to move to the next camp in the Philippines where we studied English and American culture. My husband sent me letters and money and four months later, the paperwork finally processed, Danh and I arrived in Boston, Massachusetts on July 27, 1982. There was my husband Tai Tan Dong. He was waiting for us at the gate, all dressed up and looking thinner. He picked up our son and cried.

My husband studied full-time at Wentworth Institute of Technology and worked part-time at Legal Seafood. A week after my arrival, I attended the International Institute in Boston to study English. Three months afterwards I passed ESL and went to Bunker Hill Community College. They suggested I study childhood development since I had earned a teaching degree in Vietnam, but I also took culinary arts to be sure I could get a job in a restaurant as a cook, if necessary. Danh attended school and a year later, 1984, my second son was born. We named him Vinh, which means Victory.

After my husband graduated, he began working full-time as an electrician, and I began my days by bringing Danh to the school bus, Vinh to the baby sitters, and then I went to Bunker Hill and worked part-time at the school library. I worked and studied and since we only had one car, I had to do everything by myself. I didn't understand things, and often I just came home and cried.

In September of 1985, while looking through the Boston Globe, I found a job working as a Vietnamese tutor in a Lawrence public school, so that's how we moved to Lawrence, Massachusetts. My husband found a job at Digital in Lowell and I continued my education at Merrimack College. Unlike in Boston, though, we had no friends. So I volunteered at the Asian Center and joined that community. Still, it was not enough for me.

Every weekend, my husband and I would look for some work to do, and when an old friend from Dorchester came to visit, we began planning to start a grocery store. Our friend would manage the store on the weekdays, and on the weekends and holidays, my husband and I would take over. We would call the store Tan Chau Market in honor of our hometown. Since it would be our first business, we met with a counselor at University of Massachusetts, Lowell, who guided us through the loan application process.

We opened the store in 1989. George Bush was president, the economy was slow, and our business did not do well. Soon, our friend pulled out, and since everything was in my and my husband's names, we had to take on the loan payments and property taxes. At the end of the year I decided to quit my tutoring job and manage the grocery store full-time.

Now, my husband is a support engineer at Celestica in Salem, New Hampshire. My older son, Danh, graduated from Harvard University and is working as a computer consultant. My younger son, Vinh, is heading into his third year at Boston University. And after a little more than a decade of hard work, the Tan Chau Market and Laundromat are well-established.

T. Le

Born 1933

Translated by Le-Hang Le

In 1953, the French Army was still in Vietnam, but they allowed the Vietnamese to organize their own army. At the time, we were fighting the Communists, who were trying to conquer the French, and all young adult males had to enter the military. Like most, I wanted to fight the Communists, but because I was the only son in the family, I was afraid to go directly into the battlefield. So rather than be assigned a branch of the military, I decided to select it myself and chose the Air Force. The Air Force required that you have Tu Tai I, which means that you had to graduate from high school in the eleventh grade. I had Tu Tai I, and I was the only one in the twenty young men who took the examination to be accepted.

I studied for six months, was transferred to Nha Trang to learn how to fix airplanes, and then I was transferred to Saigon to work at the Tan Son Nhat airport. I fixed the single-engine French fighter planes called Sky Raiders. The French did not allow the Vietnamese to fly the big planes, but some flew the small planes. There was one famous Vietnamese pilot, however, named Pham Phu Quoc, who died bombing Hanoi. There is a song about him.

Once the French withdrew in 1954, after Dien Bien Phu, Vietnam became a republic and we ran the airport on our own. The French did not leave completely, though; they took a group of Vietnamese back to France for training and some French officers also stayed in Vietnam to supervise and advise the Vietnamese Air Force, so eventually we were flying the C47 Dakota, the Sky Raiders and the L19 spy planes.

By1957, I was bored with my job. The work was dirty and hard. And even though we voted in Ngo Dinh Diem as President in 1956, I was worried about the state of the country. In 1958 I attended the school for intelligence called Cay Mai. Once I graduated, I became a squadron leader for a squad of twelve. I was like a go-between. The lower level soldiers tortured, interrogated and took information from captured Communist sympathizers. I signed the papers and sent the information to the head of Intelligence. Mostly we'd impound banners and flags and flyers. And in interrogations we'd find out where they hid their weapons. Even so, there were only three men I trusted in my squad. I did not know who was good or bad, exactly; I just had to remain alert.

I wore civilian clothes and lived in the villages with the people. Often, I entered the temples because at the time many Buddhist nuns and monks were spying for the Communists. My mission was not to disturb the peace, but only to look for the Communist spies who used the temples for cover. If I found them, I only followed them and reported what I saw to the higher authorities.

Sometimes, I wore the black clothing to look like the Communists, and my squad would enter villages at night in the trucks we called GMCs. The GMCs would drop us off, regardless of whether it was raining or flooding, and would not return until morning. Then we'd lie on the ground under a dark green poncho and hide that way in ambush. When we saw a person walk by, we'd order them to stop. If the person was a civilian, he'd just talk, if he was a Communist, he'd usually start shooting and then we'd all jump out.

The Communists hid inside holes in the ground, and one time, in the Saigon suburb of Binh Hung Hoa, I lay down to hide right next to one. One of the V.C. inside stuck a gun out of it and started shooting. I thought it was coming from someone in my squad, so I said, "Why'd you do that?" But once I realized what was going on, I ordered all of us to scatter so that we could cover the area and start to search. We used a type of tool to find the hole and only one or two people would go out to use it while the rest stayed outside the area and covered them. We found two Communists down the hole, but they would not come out. So I called my commanding officer, and he ordered me to keep watch there until morning, and then they sent in a reconnaissance unit. They broke open the hole, found the two Communists and said if they didn't come up they'd throw in a grenade. Finally, the two of them came out and were taken back to the base for interrogation.

Another time, we were hiding in ambush, and a horse and cart went by with five people riding in the back. They were wearing civilian clothes, so we thought they were just going to market. But then one of them must have heard a noise because all of a sudden they jumped out and started shooting, so we jumped out and shot back. Once they saw they were outnumbered, though, they retreated. But later on they met up with and were killed by the armed civilian group called the Nhan Dan Tu Ve.

My squad also once mistakenly killed a civilian. He didn't have any identification papers, and we thought he was a Communist. His family came out and said, "That man is my son! That man is my nephew!" And then they took the body away. After that the people hung my name on trees and called for my arrest because I was the leader of the squad. When I was young, I looked half French and half Vietnamese. Because of that, the townspeople around there called me Ba Lai. Ba means the third born in the family and Lai means half French and half Vietnamese. The head of the village invited me to a dinner. He said it was in honor of the Ba Lai because the Ba Lai is so kind and good. He also sent some beautiful women to me to lure me to that party, but I resisted. I had been trained to be suspicious. I knew it was a trap.

There was also a gang named the Son Dao. They weren't Communist sympathizers. The San Dao took bribes from store owners and associated with the rich. They were like the Mafia. They said they wanted to kill the Ba Lai, just for the glory.

After the Americans withdrew from Vietnam in 1973, I still did not believe we were going to lose the war. Even on April 30, 1975, when General Duong Van Minh announced on radio and television that we had to surrender, I still believed that if we could fight just one or two more days we would win.

The Communists moved into the cities and the towns and in the last week of April 1975, they moved in on the airport. On April

29, I waited with my family to be evacuated. We planned to fly to an American aircraft carrier which would have taken us to the U.S. We watched as the two planes that took off just before ours were shot down, so we didn't go.

My son was also in the Air Force, and he'd driven a GMC from Pleiku to meet us at the Saigon airport. My son used to drive planes. Now he drives a tricycle—the kind they use for taxis in Saigon.

I married in 1953 and had my first son in 1954. I had eleven children. Three died in infancy, and I had a daughter who died when she was three. While I worked in Intelligence we lived in the Air Force apartments at the airport and I owned four houses that I'd rented to Americans. But after the Americans withdrew, the apartments remained vacant. When Communists took over, they evicted us from military housing and took three of my four houses. So we moved into the one house I had left.

It was a known fact that the Communists liked three things: radios, bicycles and watches. So from April until August of 1975 I made a living by buying used watches to clean, fix and then sell. They particularly liked the watches that we say, "drove themselves," since there is no word in Vietnamese for automatic. And they liked the kind that had two lights and two windows for the date and month. If the watches were waterproof, I'd put them in a bucket of water to demonstrate that the "watch did not drown." Sometimes, just to survive, I had to sell watches I knew were pretty bad, and if one broke, I'd have to hide from the Communist I'd sold it to, by moving from market to market.

Then, one day the Communists announced over a loudspeaker that everyone who had been a former soldier for the South Vietnamese army had to turn themselves in at the Truong Vinh Ky School. They said we would be taken to a re-education camp for seven days, and then we'd be able to return to our families. So that night I walked with a group of men to the school. There, at around midnight, we were arrested, handcuffed in pairs and ordered to board a truck. We sat in the truckbed, and four Communist soldiers stood one in each corner with AK47s pointed at our heads. They covered the entire truck in canvas so it was very dark and hot, but we could breathe. A few people took their keys and cut holes in the canvas to see where we were going, and I heard some people whisper that we were being taken to the North.

I was very scared. I thought if the Communists wanted us re-educated, why would they be handcuffing us, putting guns to our heads and hiding us under canvas? Why wouldn't they want us to be comfortable? After about an hour we stopped, and they opened the canvas and called us off truck by truck; in the dark, it was hard to know how many trucks there were but when the sun rose, I saw hundreds and hundreds of people; and I saw that we were surrounded by a high fence topped with coiled razor wire. I saw rows of barracks that were completely made of metal, no windows, just doors on either end, and when they led sixty of us into one of them, I saw that we didn't have beds, just grass mats that we put down on a dirt floor. That's when I knew for sure that we were really at a prison.

We had been taken thirty kilometers north to a prison camp called Bien Hoa. No trial, no sentence, no date of release. I was imprisoned for eight years, nine months and twenty-one days and I never knew in all that time what would happen to me from one day to the next.

Once they'd taken us inside the barracks, they took off our handcuffs. An officer sat at a table by the door and called us up, one by one. Like most of them, this officer was young, about thirty years old, and wore the dark green Communist uniform. He told us the more truthful our story, the sooner we'd go home.

At noon everyone took a break, and we all got together and chose three people to go to the kitchen to ask for food. They returned with ten bowls of rice for sixty people, that was six people for one bowl of rice. Along with the rice we ate some cooked pumpkin with salt and a little bit of monosodium glutamate. The Communists really liked MSG. They didn't have it in the North, so when they discovered it in the South they loved it, and the price went up from one hundred to a thousand dong, about twenty cents to a dollar a pound.

After lunch they called the rest of us up, and at night they locked the door and left, posting guards on the outside of the barracks and in four guard towers. That first night, we all talked, everyone wondering about our future. We were sad and homesick, but we had to bear up.

The barracks were numbered, and the Communists chose one out of the group of sixty to be a group leader and another to be the leader's assistant. The Communists asked me to be a leader, but I didn't want to work for the Communists in any way and alienate myself from the others, so I refused, and they just asked someone else.

The leader listened to the grievances of the group, and if a person was sick, the leader would have to report him to the authorities. If we had to meet with a prison authority, the leader would escort us to an officer, and then an officer would escort us to the authority. The leaders could go in and out of the office. They had more air to breathe, but they didn't get any extra food or anything. Their only privilege was to be able to sleep by the door.

For latrines, they'd cut an old oil drum lengthwise, then they'd placed the two halves right in the barracks with us, and that's where we had to urinate and defecate. The smell was terrible. We called them the "refrigerators" as a kind of joke and said to the person who had to sleep next to one that he had to "hug the refrigerator." We rotated. Each person had to sleep next to the "refrigerator" for a month.

We divided into groups of six, and every day we had an assignment. Some would carry rice from the truck to the kitchen or some would weed the fields to grow pumpkins, corn and rau muong, which is a green, like spinach. In the beginning there weren't enough vegetables to feed everyone, so the officers had to buy extra at the market. One group also had to clean the latrines. They had handles at each end and two of us would grab an end and carry it outside to the two big holes we'd dug in a field. One was for feces and one was for urine. We'd also dug two wells, one by the kitchen for drinking water and one out in the field. So we'd take water from the field well and use it to wash out the latrines. The holes were filled with worms and flies. The barracks was also overrun with rats. They'd crawl over us and bite our ears and toes.

If you were old or if you were sick, you could get permission from the nurse to spend the day in the kitchen killing flies. It was like taking a sick day at work. Sometimes we pretended we were sick by saying to the nurse that we had a headache or stomach ache, something she couldn't detect, because killing flies in the kitchen was much more preferable to working in the fields. You'd put a bowl of rice water on the floor to attract them and then you'd kill them with a swatter. Some prisoners though, would just sit in the kitchen and rest and maybe ask the cook for leftovers. Since the cooks were also prisoners, they were usually sympathetic, but one time the cooks reported them, and the authorities ordered those prisoners to kill two hundred flies a day.

Everyone got dysentery. And some had thought ahead and brought with them some medicine. A friend of mine had brought some too, which saved me. Not that many people died in Bien Hoa, but many died in the next camp they sent me to, which was Phu Quoc Island. Then I went to Long Giao. Ham Tan was the worst, though. My imprisonment at Ham Tan was the most difficult time in my life.

Ham Tan was controlled by the police. The rules there were strict, and if anyone violated them they were beaten or tortured. Once I was so sick there that I couldn't work, and the police and four prisoners put me on a stretcher and carried me out to lie under a tree while everyone else worked. The police stood around me to harass and brainwash me, saying things like, "Why are you sick? Do you want to go home?" Saying things just to make me angry and agitated. At one point one of them put a gun to my head and said, "I could kill you with this, but I'd rather save the bullet. You're life isn't worth a bullet." Many people died, one person a day—of starvation and disease and from hard labor and poor nutrition. In Phuoc Long we'd have to take out the dead, build a coffin and bury them. Then the prisoner's family would come, but we would not be able to speak with them.

In Bien Hoa and Phu Quoc we could not have visitors. In Long Giao we could have visitors every two months, but if our family did not have enough means to get there, then we'd have no visitors. Even if my wife came, we couldn't speak, because a guard would sit right next to us. I saw my ten-year-old daughter once, but they wouldn't let me hug her. And while I was in prison my three-year-old daughter died, but my wife didn't tell me. I learned three years later. I had asked my wife to bring her to visit me, but she kept saying she was too young and would be too tired. I learned of my daughter's death from another prisoner who was a neighbor of mine, and whose wife had told him when she'd visited.

We could write letters home every two months. Of course all the guards would read them, and if you wrote, "I miss you and I don't know when I'm coming home," and if you asked for sugar and fat, the foods we really needed, the soldiers would say the letter was too romantic, and we could be beaten. The Communists would also open and read all the letters our families sent to us. They'd use them for toilet paper, so sometimes we'd find them lying in the fields. I didn't care if they were smeared with excrement. I'd pick one up to see who it was from and I'd be happy if it was for me. If the letter was for someone else, I'd be sure to find him and give it to him.

We'd work like cattle and bathe in the dirty streams, and this was why people got sick so easily. When the female prisoners took baths they only had male guards to watch them, so they'd tell the guards to turn their faces, "You wouldn't watch your mother bathe, would you?" they said. The female prisoners had more power than the male prisoners. Sometimes they went on strike and refused to work, without any consequences from the Communists. Their leader was a female prisoner who had been a colonel in the South Vietnamese army. They made flyers and replicas of the former flag, and they'd tie them onto the tails of rats, so the rats would disperse them out into the village. When the male prisoners passed their barracks, they'd shout at us that we were timid and cowards and not strong enough to stand up to the Communists. The Communists didn't like it, and eventually they transferred the women to another camp.

I was called up to be released on September 2, 1984, but because it was a national holiday, my release was delayed, and I had to go to the jungle for ten more days to cut bamboo and palm leaves. Finally, on September 12, I got my release papers, five dong, enough for a day's worth of food, and walked out of the camp with some other prisoners who'd also been released. We walked to a market, and the people there gave us some vegetables, and two women called some truck drivers and paid for our fare back to Saigon.

When I came home, my adult children recognized me, but my youngest daughter, Tram, did not. She was embarrassed and didn't know if she could call me "Dad."

I took care of the children while my wife continued to make a living selling used clothing and appliances and furniture. I was on probation for a year, which meant that I had to report everything I did to the police, where I went, who I met with. I was angry and disappointed and hopeless. I had no freedom, restricted even in my own home. And when I went out, the police would follow me. When I was young, I'd been ordained to be a Buddhist monk, so to give me some peace, I chanted the Sutra every morning and every night.

One time, while I was chanting in the evening, a police officer wearing civilian clothes knocked on the door. My wife answered and asked him, "Who are you and what do you want?" He barged in the house and said to me, "Next time I knock, stop chanting and answer the door yourself. Don't have your wife come out and interrogate me!" The officer was my son's age, and he spoke to me so disrespectfully. It infuriated me.

Eventually, the Communists gave us some concessions. I found out that if you were imprisoned more than three years, you could apply to immigrate to any country, but mostly to the U.S. I didn't believe it at first. I waited. I had believed them when they told me I was just going to go to a re-education camp for seven days, and instead they'd sent me to prison for eight years, so I was afraid to believe anything again. But after my friend applied, he urged me to apply too. He said I was too timid. He said, "So if we're arrested, we can go to jail together again!"

Finally, I gave in. It took three tries. I had to go to the District Office at three a.m. to wait in line. They processed one hundred applications a day. Some people slept there overnight so that when the doors opened, they could be the first person in line. I had to buy the application for

20,000 dong, about $1.50.

I filled out the application in 1986. Nine years later, my wife, my youngest daughter and I arrived in Florida. The person who sponsored us, though, was a Methodist and made us go to church with him. And he was disrespectful to us. He made us sleep on the kitchen floor.

My wife and daughter were crying every day, so I called my older daughter who'd been living in Lowell, Massachusetts since 1994. I asked her if we could travel there to live with her. She said the weather was too cold there, and we would not be comfortable. But I waited for sale-price plane tickets to Boston, asked a friend to buy them for us, and called my daughter from Logan airport to tell her to come pick us up.

I became a citizen in 2000 and applied for Supplemental Security Income. We would like to live with our daughter and son-in-law, but my son-in-law won't allow it, so we rent an apartment. My wife and I help with our grandchildren, but my daughter and son-in-law don't pay us for it.

My wife and I are sick, and I am concerned about the cold. I don't know English and can't do a lot on my own. Luckily, I can drive though, and go to the market and the senior center and the temple. But I'm lonely and depressed. Here, though, I feel I won't be arrested, that the unexpected won't happen. In Vietnam we had too many traumas. In Vietnam we couldn't sleep.

L. Nguyen

Born 1932

Translated by Le-Hang Le

My life is similar to the weather, sometimes rainy, sometimes hot and dry.

I had a difficult childhood. My parents were very poor, so I lived with a family in the countryside who made a living by interpreting for the French. They treated my like their own child, but because of the war, they had to keep moving, and I couldn't go to school past the fifth grade. When I turned eighteen, I went to Saigon, worked as a vendor in the market, and went to school at night to learn to read and write in Vietnamese and to study French. I rented an apartment in the same building as my husband, Mr. Le, and asked him to help me with my homework. That's how we met.

When my husband was in the Air Force, I stayed home to take care of the children. I would carry the baby to the market, buy food and come home and cook for the family. When I went out, the older children would stay home with the younger children. I accepted my life, but I was not that happy. It was crowded in Air Force housing. I wanted to start a business. I don't know what kind it would have been. I just knew I wanted one, but my children were too young and I had to take care of them instead. Every two years I had one child, from 1954 to 1975, eleven children in all, but four died.

On April 25, 1975, I had to move out of the Air Force housing. Because we couldn't be evacuated, I took the younger of my seven children and went to my parents' house. The older children stayed at the apartment to try and save it. Five days later, I returned with the younger children, hoping I could move back in, but the Communist soldiers would not let me. They didn't threaten to kill me or anything, they just said that I had to go, that I had to move out immediately, so we all moved to the one house we owned that the Communists had not taken.

At first I just stayed home. I had no spirit. I wasn't scared. I didn't feel anything, but I still got up and fed and took care of my children. The house was furnished, so in the beginning we sold all the furniture in the house to a buyer from the market. The buyer was then going to sell it at a higher price at the market, and that's how I came to do the same thing. After I sold everything we owned, I went out, bought things from people, and I began selling them at the market too. My husband bought watches, then cleaned and sold them. People would come in from the countryside, buy our things in the city, then return to the countryside to sell it to the villagers. Some bought things to sell to the soldiers.

The Communists wouldn't allow people to sell used furniture and clothing in the market. Sometimes they'd come, surround the market and shoot in the sky. Then they'd arrest us, load us all into trucks and take us to jail from eight a.m. one day to four p.m. the next. The jail had once been someone's house. It would be too crowded there to lie down. We had bathrooms, but we did not get anything to eat the whole time. My children would be at home—four of them were going to school—and they would not know where I was. They would just wait and take care of each other.

Once I was doing business in central Vietnam. I went there to sell watches, used clothes and machines to the highland people. From the highland people I'd buy corn, coffee, tobacco and hot peppers to sell in Saigon. Tobacco and coffee were particularly valuable, so I'd tie them to my legs to hide them under my pants. Still, the police stopped and frisked me and so found and took the coffee and tobacco. They even took the rings from my fingers.

Whenever I was arrested, I'd lose all of my property too, so I would only put some of it in a bag and take it from home to display at the market. Sometimes I'd hide it in a bag under my arm, but the police would grab that away too. I had to live like this for nine years, but the government didn't provide enough jobs for the people, so it was my only choice. I was arrested four or five times over nine years, and every time I lost all of my property. It makes me suffer to remember it.

There really weren't any rules. When I brought food to my husband in prison, they would take a chopstick and stir it around in the rice to see if I was hiding contraband. Sometimes the police went into my house and searched it without giving me any explanation. The Communists had said that all families could only have three pairs of clothes. But we didn't follow that rule, so their house searches made me very afraid. They called anyone who'd been in the South Vietnamese military "puppets of the former regime," and they harassed us even more than others.

One day the soldiers came to my house and told me that I had to move my family to the New Economy Zone. But I refused. Instead, I divided my family in two. I sent my son and his wife and children, and I stayed with the rest of the family, so that I would not lose the house. The New Economy Zone was fifty miles away and in the forest. My son had to live in a house made of bamboo poles and a thatched roof, a house that storms would destroy. And people in the New Economy Zone had to work hard cutting down the forest and planting vegetables. My son and his family didn't have enough food to eat, so I would leave the eight-month-old baby and the three-year-old in my older children's care, and I would leave to take them rice, fish sauce and dry, salted fish. First I would take a bus, and then I would walk a half hour into the forest, carrying the food on both my shoulders.

I also carried food to my husband in prison, and I saved the money I made at the market to buy sugar, pork fat and bran from the rice—something pigs would eat. But I mixed it with the lemon juice, sugar, and bran and then baked it into a cake for my husband to eat.

One time when I was gone, my three year old daughter, Le Ngoc Thanh, fell off a wall in front of our house. Her head swelled up, and my older daughter, Tuyet, who was nineteen at the time, was afraid to tell anyone what had happened. She rubbed salt and saliva on the swelling to make it go down, but that only made it worse. Then the baby got a high fever and began to vomit. That's when I came home and took her in a taxi to the hospital. The doctors inserted an I.V., and whatever was in it shocked the baby and she died.

The neighbors helped buy the wood and made the coffin. I had to go to three different offices before the Communists granted me a piece of burial land. We rented a three-wheeled Lambro car to carry the coffin to the cemetery. Because I could visit so infrequently, my husband found out about the baby's death before I could tell him.

Because I was often gone, Le Ngoc Thanh was more attached to Tuyet, my older daughter, than she was to me. And when Le ngoc Thanh died, Tuyet began to act possessed. She'd call out to the baby, and sometimes she'd suddenly go into the Lotus position and rock back and forth. My husband took her to different temples and healers to try to help her. The first healer said that if he poured boiling water over her and she was not harmed by it, she was possessed. He poured the water, and no harm came to her. He also lit rose petals and said if she was possessed, the smoke would not blacken or burn her face, and it didn't. Still, though, she did not get better. But the last healer she visited told the baby's spirit to leave Tuyet alone and stay there with him. He said, "I will care for you. Let your sister go on with her life." He put pictures of the baby on his altar, and he offered food to her there. After that, Tuyet improved. She lives in Lowell now, and she is still grateful to the healer. She sends him money sometimes to help him care for the spirit of her younger sister.

On the night of September 12, 1984, my husband arrived home from prison. He knocked on the door, and the children heard and recognized his voice. They came out and he hugged them and they cried. But I just sat still. I had no feeling. I didn't even cry. Now I don't have enough tears to cry.

After some years, life became better. The police stopped arresting me, and I could build a booth and open more of a shop at the market. But I had to pay a tax for it every month to a civilian tax collector. The collector estimated what I made each month and took a percentage based on his estimation, then took a cut himself and gave the rest to the government. There were also more rules. I had to put a price tag on all my items. If I didn't, the police would confiscate them. You could still bargain, though. Sometimes I would have to settle on a cheap price, just to have some money to feed my children.

When we heard we could apply to come to America, I wanted to go. I had heard how in America people went to school and had a good life. I wanted my youngest daughter to come here and be educated. I wanted her to have a bright future. But my life had been so hard, I did not expect very much for myself.

In America I feel safer. My life is comfortable. I have enough money to survive. I go to a school across the street to learn English, but I can never remember the vocabulary. I don't drive, but the market is nearby, and sometimes I walk there by myself. I don't miss very much about Vietnam. Four of my children are still there though, so it's my children I miss.

Seeds of Lotus: Cambodian and Vietnamese Voices in America

Huong Tu

Born 1965

Translated by Hue Nguyen

When I lived in Saigon, I went to a French school from kindergarten to first grade. It was probably for the more wealthy families. My father took me there everyday on his motor scooter. I stood in front of him on the floor of the Vespa. And before he dropped me off, we would eat breakfast in a Saigon restaurant. Then he would go to work at the American Embassy. He was an accountant and he spoke English.

For two years, my father gave money to the authorities to stay out of the army, but the third year, in 1972, they made him go. That meant that my mother had to go to work, and there wouldn't be anyone to take care of the children. I was eight, my sister Phuc was four, my brother Loi was two and my other brother Loc was eight months old. My parents sold our house in the Third District, in the center of Saigon. I was very sad. I didn't know much about the war. I only knew my father was going away into the army.

We put our furniture in a rental truck and moved three hours out of the city to my grandmother's house in the countryside, which was in the Sa Dec Province. My grandmother owned land that she rented to farmers. Her house had a kitchen, one big living room and one big bedroom. The house was near the market, so other houses were close by. Farther from the market the houses were more spread out. The roof and walls were made of tin sheets, so it was very, very hot. In the city we had faucets, but in the country I had to carry water in buckets from the river. There was no electricity, only oil lamps, so it was also very dark, and I was afraid of ghosts.

My mother only stayed with us for one month. Then she and my baby brother moved back to the city where my mother worked making food like noodles and sticky rice for children's breakfasts that she sold in front of the schools, and she lived in a rented apartment. I didn't miss my mother that much. I missed my father more than my mother.

My little sister wasn't as familiar as I was with my grandmother, and I remember one day she wanted to go to school with me. I had to lie to her and said I was just going to get something and that I would be right back. After school, when I came home, my little sister was still standing at the door. She had stood there and waited for me for five hours.

At school, the children liked to play with the "city girl," and the teacher also liked me, the "city girl." And at home, my grandmother gave me jobs to do. She made vinegar from banana and coconut water. About once a week I had to carry in each hand a five litre bottle, about a gallon and a half of vinegar, to a store near the market. It took about twenty minutes to walk to the store. Once, my grandmother made iced tea and asked me to sell it at the bus station. She didn't tell me that I would have to yell: "Iced tea! Iced tea for sale!" like all the other children there doing the same thing. They sold out all their iced tea and even sold it on the buses, but I was too scared. I just stood there from the morning to the afternoon with the iced tea at my feet and didn't say a word. No one bought any of it, of course, and I took it all home again. The next morning I didn't want to go back, and I never went again.

At night we all slept together in the one big bedroom. My grandmother slept with my brother in one bed, and my sister and I slept in another bed. At around eleven o'clock, about three times a week, we'd hear the bombs. The noise was very loud, really big booms, and it would shake the house and wake everyone up. But I never got into the sandbag bomb shelter, though I remember seeing my grandmother there. She always sat in front of it, though, never inside. My brother, sister and I just sat on our beds. I would be very scared for my father and pray.

In the morning, I would take a short walk from my grandmother's house to the corner to watch for the wounded soldiers. Not a lot of other children watched, just adults, and I usually stood by myself to see South Vietnamese soldiers, not American, lying in the backs of open trucks, being taken to a hospital from the forests and jungles of Dong Thap Muoi, about three miles away. The roads were bumpy and covered with rocks and the trucks would move by very slowly, usually about three of them. Fifteen minutes and one would come out, then another fifteen minutes and another would go by and then another. Mostly I saw leg and arm injuries. I would see the blood, and sometimes I'd see the soldiers' relatives riding with them in the backs of the trucks, crying.

My father was in the army for three months. He saw his friend get wounded right in front of him. He carried him out of the battle on his shoulders and brought him to a field hospital, but the next morning his friend died. My father visited my grandmother for one day, and then he went back to the city to visit my mother. At the same time, he saw that a company needed an accountant, so he applied and got the job and was home again. But still, my parents stayed together in the city with my youngest brother, Loc. My grandmother didn't want the rest of us to go back to the city because we didn't own a house anymore. In Vietnam most people own their houses, they don't rent as much as they do here. So, when my father came back, my mother continued to work, and my father was working and since there was still no one to take care of my brother and sister and me, we lived with my grandmother for two more years, until the war ended.

I had always wanted to go back to the city, and one month after the war ended, I finally did.

Seeds of Lotus: Cambodian and Vietnamese Voices in America

Hue Nguyen

Born 1956

Written by Hue Nguyen

To my parents who sacrificed everything to save money for us to escape. And to my dear sisters and brothers.

Before 1975, my father worked as a nurse in a hospital. My mother owned a sewing machine store. They had eleven children. After 1975, my father retired, and my mother had to close her store because the Communist government controlled all the businesses and factories. Each city or province had a cooperative commissary that sold food daily for the people. People stood on long lines to get basic supplies. The schools closed so that the government could change the curriculum to suit the Communist theories.

From 1975 until 1982, no one could open their own store to earn a living. Everything belonged to the government. All families had a difficult time earning a living. One night at dinner my father said, "Your mother and I have already experienced living under the Communist regime in North Vietnam. Even if you graduate from college and work very hard, you will never have enough money to buy food. That's why your mother and I escaped to the South. Now we have to find ways for all of you to escape the country. One by one you will leave and that means I will not allow any of you to date or marry." None of us said a word.

From 1976 on, my brothers, sisters and I began to look for ways to escape. In the meantime we all continued attending school. My parents spent the money that they had saved to buy us food and school supplies, and we were very lucky. Most of my friends had to drop out and earn money by working on farms.

We heard a lot of bad news. People cheated each other to get money and gold. A lot of people who tried to escape died, were raped or were caught and sent to jail for two or three years. But a few people succeeded. People who lived in villages had a greater chance of succeeding than city people like us. My parents had to pay fifteen hundred to two thousand dollars in advance for each attempt. If we succeeded on the first try, my parents would pay the rest, another fifteen hundred dollars. If we failed we would be able to try a few more times for the same fee. If we got caught and sent to jail, the money would be gone with the wind.

In 1979 two of my brothers tried escaping month after month and finally succeeded after almost one and a half years of trying. They escaped in a motorboat filled with four hundred and fifty people. They were told to board the boat with only what they wore. They could not take any bags, and they could not take any water. Fifty people died. They threw the bodies to the sharks. My younger brother, dying from dehydration, was also nearly thrown overboard too. But then they were rescued by an American naval ship in the Thailand Sea. After that, one by one, my family continued to try to escape.

Between 1980 and 1986, I was teaching at a middle school in Saigon. I tried to escape on my vacation weeks or in the summer so that I could still keep my job. Sometimes I went with my younger sister, sometimes I went with the older one, but we always failed. In all, we made eleven attempts. Each one made a deep impression on my life. I try not to remember, but I always do.

In 1985, before I tried to escape with my younger sister, my mother said to me and my sister, "If you want to escape, you're going to have to leave soon. You have to get ready, but if you don't want to go, let me know."

I said, "I want to."

My parents had two houses, one that they lived in, in the tenth district, and one for all of my sisters in the third district. The night before I left, my sister and I stayed at my sisters' house. I didn't want my mom to cry because tears bring bad luck. I packed only a black suit, five Tylenol pills, ten Vitamin C pills and I sewed fifty dollars into the seam of my jacket. My sister did the same.

We left the house early in the morning and took a commercial truck to Ba Ria Province at one p.m. My sister and I had lunch in a restaurant and stayed there for two hours. At three o'clock, the leader arrived. He was a young man, about twenty-five years old. I had met him on the previous day in front of my district's school, so I recognized him right away. He didn't say anything. He just guided us through the deserted streets of a small village. The village had some small scattered houses in it. We entered one of them and saw there, a grandmother, mother, and a son and daughter. My sister and I hid in a small dark back room behind a curtain that separated us from the front. Later, two boys joined us and while we waited, I said the Rosary. We had dinner, but I was too nervous to eat.

It was around ten o'clock at night when we finally left. The leader said, "Please don't talk. Just follow me. I'm going to walk fast." There were four people in the group, my sister and me and the two boys. It was very dark. There were no moon or stars in the sky, and it was so quiet I could hear the sound of the crickets and cicadas and the wind moving the leaves. The path leading to the river was full of puddles and so rough that I nearly fell a number of times. The whole time my mouth muttered prayers to St. Martin. I still remember those prayers, now.

Finally, we reached the riverbank and got into a rowboat, five of us in all. The captain who steered the boat with one pole, the two boys sitting on the right side and me and my sister on the left. The water was calm. It would take two hours to get to the big motorboat that would take us the rest of the way. Nobody said anything. I prayed to the Virgin Mary and St. Martin. Suddenly, I heard something moving, then very clearly heard the sound of a boat's motor. It was moving toward us. Our guide quickly jerked our boat in another direction, hard enough to make it rock. I almost fell into the river. With the pole in his hand, he pushed us to the riverbank and said, "Get out! Get out! I have to hide my boat."

"We don't know how to swim," I said.

He didn't answer. Suddenly, he just tilted the boat close to the bushes and I fell overboard. I reached out to grab the side of the boat, but it was gone and I was sure I would drown. It was very dark, but I could make out my sister who was standing next to me in the light from the fireflies, and I felt better.

My God! Where was this place, I thought. The riverbank was covered with bushes and thorny plants. And I was not in water. I was standing in something like the cake batter I made with eggs, milk, butter and flour. It was up to my chest, up to my sister's waist and up to the boys' chins. To keep our balance, we grabbed onto some overhanging branches, and whenever I tried to move to a better place, I just sank deeper. I remembered the novel, Papillon, about a prisoner escape and recalled from that, that it was very dangerous to move in a swamp. If we tried to walk, I realized, we would die.

I whispered, "Don't move, Huong," I said to my sister, "Tell the boys not to move. Just wait here and pray."

The boys didn't listen, though. Maybe they were too afraid of being caught.

I was cold and exhausted. All I could do was stand there with more than half my body in the mud, holding onto the branches while mosquitoes and other insects bit my face and arms and hands. I heard the sound of waves hitting the sides of a motorboat out at sea and I thought, at least if I got caught I'd be out of this situation. One more second and I felt I would just let go and give up, but still, we waited. I looked at my sister. Her situation was a little better. She was not as deeply stuck in the mud, but she still had to hold onto the branches. I shook my head and said, "Please continue praying to St. Martin." She didn't answer.

Then the leader came back. He couldn't draw near enough to us for us to climb in from where we were, so we had to walk on tiptoe, about twenty feet out into the river to reach him. When I was close enough, he pulled me up by my hand. Next was my sister. Then the man whistled for the boys, but we didn't hear anything back. We waited for them for almost a half an hour. Then the captain told us, "They could have never made it out. It's too deep and muddy."

Back on shore the mud weighed me down. We took a shortcut to the guide's house to quickly wash it off, then right away, we left. I had lost my bag and shoes, so we boarded a bus barefoot and got home at four a.m. The neighborhood was quiet. Everybody was still in bed.

We prayed for a miracle for the boys, but the next day the leader and the boys' mother came to my house to get information. They cried, and I cried too. They asked, "Do you remember where you were? Can you help us find their bodies?"

I had no idea where we were, I told them. "You should ask the captain. Maybe he will take you over there." I felt very sad for them. They left my house with no more information than when they'd come.

I heard the boys had died and though they'd looked for their bodies in secret, they never found them. After that, we stopped escaping from that province.

My next attempt was also with my older sister in 1986. This time we went to another province called Bac Lieu. It took seven hours to get there in a commercial truck. We arrived at four in the afternoon. We were nervous the whole time. In the years from 1975 to 1990, if you wanted to leave for the countryside, you had to fill out a form and get permission from the local police station. We didn't apply for permission because my three brothers were already living in the U.S.A., so we didn't want them to suspect that we were escaping. Most people didn't apply either. But we didn't look like the people from that province. Just one moment of inattention and we could get caught. As city people, it was easy for us to go to jail.

The leader, who was also a young man in his early twenties, came to guide us to the secret house so that at night we could walk to the river. There were four people in the group, a lady with her three-year-old son, my older sister, and I. The leader seemed to know the area very well. He walked confidently. We didn't talk to each other, not even one word, just followed him in a single line. I had to look at his back every second so as not to lose him. Sometimes I had to run to keep up with him. We followed him for about thirty minutes and then suddenly he disappeared. I didn't know what happened. Maybe it wasn't safe to walk like that, or he recognized a policeman in civilian clothes. He just left us in the middle of the road.

I thought, should I go forward or back? Where are we going? What could we say to a policeman at this time of night? It was eight p.m. It was getting darker and darker. Oh my God. I started praying to St. Martin. Suddenly, my sister turned around and walked quickly away. I just followed her and didn't say a thing for about fifteen minutes. She asked me, "Hue, didn't you see the village police station in front of us?"

"No," I said. "You know I'm near-sighted!"

We wandered for about fifteen minutes more and then saw a boy who was about ten years old. He carried a lantern and a fishing pole, on his way to do some night fishing. We followed him for a while to find a deserted place. I asked him if there was an inn around. He said, "The government won't allow inns to accept people after five p.m."

Then I asked, "Where's the commercial truck station?"

"It's near here," he said. "It takes about fifteen minutes to get there."

So that's where we went. It was getting darker and darker. I could barely see the street. We knew, in order to be safe, we would have to get back to Saigon that night. But when I arrived at the truck station, I heard someone say that there was no truck that night going to Saigon. We didn't have any choice. We had to sleep on the ground, next to the ticket booth.

Of course we didn't sleep for one second. There were a lot of street vendors and retailers who also needed to get to Saigon to buy goods, so it was too noisy, and we were afraid that the police would come at any minute to check IDs. The moment someone looked at us, we moved to another place. We had to be alert to everything.

At about three a.m., some young boys came by. One of them asked me if I wanted to rent a toothbrush. At first, I didn't understand. "You want to sell me a toothbrush?" I said.

"No. You can brush your teeth and then return the toothbrush to me, and then I'm going to rent it to another person," he replied.

I had never heard of anyone renting a toothbrush and was about to say no, when my older sister blinked her eyes at me. So, I said, "Okay," but I didn't use it. The brush was old and wet!

When the boy came back for the toothbrush, we moved again. He could inform the police that we were strangers.

In the morning we found out that we still couldn't buy tickets to Saigon. There were only two commercial trucks going that day. We were even ready to buy tickets for triple the standard price, but there were no more tickets for sale, so we had to wander around the Bac Lieu market all day long without resting once to close our eyes.

That night, we went back to the same truck station to again sleep on the ground next to the ticket booth, and again I couldn't sleep at all. The situation was the same as the previous night. How could anyone sleep anyway with the kind of worries I had on my mind? The next morning, we could finally buy tickets back to Saigon.

After that I was very sick. I had terrible headaches for many days from the lack of sleep.

After one month the boat owner called us again. This time they had changed locations. The launch spot was in My Tho Province. I was still too sick and terrified to go. I was afraid I wouldn't make it. Only my older sister went. It was in the middle of 1986. Just as she made it to the big boat she was arrested and was imprisoned for one and a half years. She had to work very hard cutting bamboo in the forest. I had to visit her every two weeks to provide her food. The jail was very far from the city. I got up at three a.m. and went to the truck station to buy a ticket, and I always had to buy one at the black market price.

I arrived at the jail at eleven o'clock in the morning, waited for two hours and saw my sister for only twenty minutes. I handed her the bag full of food and water, and we dared not cry in front of the officers. After eighteen months they released her, seven days before New Year's Eve. After my sister came home, all of us felt hopeless and depressed, and for six months we stopped trying to escape.

Then one of my sisters found another way out. It took only eight hours to get from Cambodia to Thailand, so we could start there. The organizer, a lady in her early forties, was very superstitious. She said,

"First, I have to ask my fortuneteller if you should go. She will make the decision." We were Catholic and didn't believe in superstition, but we had no choice.

The next day, at my house, the fortuneteller asked for our ages and the years we were born. She also looked at our hands. Finally, she told me, "You can't go this time. It's not your time." Then she turned to my second sister and said, "But you can escape. Your face is very bright; besides you were born in the Year of the Tiger. Tiger is very strong and powerful. He stands at the front door. His spirit is heavy. No one can get out. That's why the five of you can't succeed. I feel this time is for you. You must get out."

When we heard that, we were very sad. My second sister had been in jail with the family of my eldest sister's husband for a while and said she had decided not to ever try again. My other sisters and I tried to convince her, "Please try. Just one more time. We'll pray for you. Your spirit is too heavy. If you don't go, we can't go." For nearly a week she continued to refuse. She said, "If I were in jail in Cambodia, who would visit me?" No one answered, but I told her, "We'll pray for you the whole time."

On the last day, before the group departed, the fortuneteller came back and said to my second sister, "Do you want to go, or not? Don't worry. You'll succeed. Please remember, if you go, allow no one in your family to walk with you to the bus station." That night she finally decided to go and the next morning, while it was still dark outside, she left alone for the bus. I was crying from worry, and my parents didn't even know that she'd left.

Three weeks later, she sent us a telegram from Thailand. My parents couldn't believe how quickly it had happened. Two months later, the fortuneteller returned. This time, she still did not allow me and my younger sister to escape. She told my third sister, "You can go this time, but your journey will be more difficult than your sister's. You could go to jail, but you will get out and succeed. The journey was a good dream for your older sister, but it will not be for you." It was true. My third sister did succeed and met my second sister in Songkhla refugee camp in Thailand, but she'd been in jail in Cambodia for five days and she was sick. She had severe asthma and thought she wasn't going to make it. In 1992, after living in the U.S. for three and a half years, she passed away.

Two months later, in August of 1987, the fortuneteller came back again. My younger sister insisted that we go to meet up with our two sisters who were waiting for us in Thailand. The fortuneteller said, "I'm not sure if both of you can succeed, because I don't see it. Maybe you will come back to Vietnam." We didn't care. We just wanted to go.

My sister met the organizer at the bus station. This organizer was the same lady who had ensured the success of my sisters' escapes. To get to the Cambodian border we rode on a commercial truck, bus, motorcycle and walked, and once there, the organizer had a visa to pass legally into Cambodia, so she simply went on her way, and gave the responsibility of me and my sister to another leader in her group. The group in all was made up of ten people. To avoid the police, the new leader led us into the forest. It was totally dark. I held my sister's hand and she held someone else's hand to avoid getting lost, but we were far from alone. There were many people walking through the forest, most of them illegal retailers who bought goods like machines from Thailand and then, to avoid taxes, transported them back through the forest. I couldn't see them, but I could hear them talking to each other about prices and goods.

Once someone lit a flashlight and my leader ground her teeth and said, "Turn that off! If they see it, they'll shoot us!" And I did hear shots in the distance, which terrified me. Every time we heard them we had to lay down on the ground, wait about five minutes and then get up and continue on. As we approached the edge of the forest we heard more and more and sometimes they were very close and at that point I began to regret my decision to try again to escape. We could get shot so easily there, and no one would ever know. My older sister hadn't written to us about this, and I thought maybe the organizer had changed the route because the police had found out about the escapes by boat.

We walked, then rested for a half hour, then kept walking for five more hours in complete darkness. By the time we reached the road it was about three a.m., and I was too exhausted to walk anymore. I sat on the roadside to wait for a commercial truck into town while the leader divided us into smaller groups.

First, my sister and I stayed in a house in Phnom Penh, in a big house made of brick. The design was similar to those in Vietnam. The people who owned it made candies and sold them in different towns in Cambodia. We pretended to be the packing workers. I felt better, but still, I didn't want to continue. The leader kept us completely in the dark about what was next, where we were going and how we were going to get there. But how could I go back to Vietnam?

After a week, the leader came and said, "You have to move. You shouldn't stay in one house for too long." So we moved to a tiny fishing village far out of the city, so small it didn't even have a name. They called it "The Fourth Village." It had only one or two wooden houses and the rest were straw or grass huts. If it was too rainy to fish, people stayed home and gambled. They gambled everywhere and every day. At the village gate there was a night club where men drank and danced and sometimes fought over girls and shot at each other.

My sister and I lived in a Vietnamese couple's house. They were both about twenty-five years old and had a one-year-old baby girl. The wife told us, "We are very poor. My husband and I wandered from place to place and then we settled here." She was nice, but the husband was an alcoholic. Because my parents had paid $1,500 for our escape, I knew the leader must have paid the couple for our shelter and food, but the man asked us for money anyway. I knew he'd use it to buy alcohol, so the first time I said no. "Well," he said, "Then tomorrow, we won't have any money for food. So we'll eat only rice." For two days that's what we were given, rice and water. How could we continue on without any food, I thought? Still, I knew if I gave him money, he'd only ask for more. What could I do? I gave in. The next time he asked, I gave him some money, and sure enough he didn't give it to his wife to buy food, he went out and got drunk. Then he came home red-faced, threw things on the floor and yelled at his wife.

At night, the strong wind puffed the straw roof. It was cold and I didn't have a blanket. In one corner the couple fought and yelled at each other and the baby cried. In the other corner my sister and I just sat there. With nothing to divide the house we couldn't possibly sleep, and if we did, we took turns, afraid of what the man might do to us. I prayed to St. Martin the whole time. "St. Martin, you even loved the animals in the field. I pray to you. Let me get out of here as soon as possible."

Finally, the leader came and said again, "We have to leave," and my sister and I took a motor tricycle ride to a deserted place. I had no idea where I was. Sixty or seventy other people were already there, standing and waiting for what, we didn't know.

Finally, a big army truck pulled up driven by two Cambodian men. They said something that I didn't understand and then gestured for us to get into the back of the truck. I was very nervous. I said, "Huong. Are we going to escape by this truck? What are they going to do with us?" She just shook her head. It was too crowded even to sit, so everyone stood, crushed together, and then the Cambodian men took a thick dark canvas tarp and covered us entirely, and as they were tying the knots, I thought that they were not leaving us any opening for air. How were we going to breathe? But they tied it too quickly for me to say anything and I didn't know any Khmer, anyway. So suddenly we found ourselves trapped.

The truck started forward on the bumpy road. No one could move, and we had nothing to grab onto. Someone fell against my back and I fell onto someone else. Then someone started yelling, "Stop! I can't breathe! I'm going to die!" Then another person yelled, and there was total chaos. I felt like fainting, like someone had covered my mouth and nose. I thought I was going to die, but then I heard a loud voice say, "Who has a knife? Anything sharp. We need to rip the canvas; otherwise we'll suffocate. So people started scratching and kicking at the canvas, but it was useless. Then, finally, a man found a big rock on the truck floor and by pushing the rock through the hole near the knot he ripped it bigger and everyone yelled and kicked the sides of the truck.

Suddenly the truck lurched to a stop and the driver climbed out, untied the canvas and everyone automatically jumped down and then the truck was gone. For a half hour or so, my sister and I wandered up and down the road. There was no sign of transportation there and the place looked like a desert. Another half hour passed and then the police arrived.

My sister and I stayed in jail for two days. I realized that some other people who'd been with us had disappeared, so I pretended to have to go to the bathroom, saw a guard, gave him some money and he let us out. My sister and I found another group of people and looked for ways to get back to Vietnam.

In January of 1988, the organizer came back to our house and said that if my sister and I did not go one more time, we would lose the money my parents had paid for the previous attempt. So once again, my sister and I made another attempt. This would be our tenth. We could not consult the fortuneteller because she and her son had already escaped.

We met the leader, a lady who spoke both Vietnamese and Khmer, at the bus station at three thirty a.m. All she said was, "Please be alert. Just follow me. The police are around. Don't ask questions." There were five people in our group: my eldest sister's friend, her two children, my sister and I. In Can Tho City only my sister and I stayed at the leader's cousin's house for two nights and then we left for Chau Doc, a province which was closer to the border of Cambodia. "From Chau Doc, we'll need to take a short trip on a rice boat to avoid the police," the leader said. "I'll have to ask them for a ride. Look at me. Pay them as much as they want. It will please them. Don't bargain. Otherwise, they will inform on us. Both of you definitely don't look like rice retailers."

I saw motorboats and rowboats, all of them on the river bank, all of them owned by people who bought, sold and transported different kinds of rice. The leader jumped nimbly from one boat to another, but it seemed that most of the owners did not want to take the risk. Finally the leader nodded at us. She'd found a boat, but unlike her I couldn't jump without falling, so they had to row the boat as close to me as possible and then I crawled from one boat to another to finally get in.

At the border I saw a Cambodian soldier holding an AK47 sitting in the blockhouse. Another soldier, also armed, was standing next to a fence. The leader said, "Stay here. I have to talk to him." She spoke to him in Khmer, and the soldier smiled and nodded. Then she waved for us to follow her. We had passed the border. It was five in the evening and rapidly getting dark. There were few houses and the leader paid three motorcycle riders to give us a lift. My sister and I climbed onto one and he drove very fast down a rough path in the forest. My hips ached and I was exhausted; Huong was, too, and must have loosened her grip because all of a sudden she fell off. I screamed into the driver's ears, "Stop! Please stop! I can't hold on. I don't think we can make it."

The leader came up to me, looked into my face and then agreed. She said there were a lot of wild animals around there, so I better be able to find a stilt house. We did find one, made of wood with ten steps up to the first floor. It was only one room and didn't seem to belong to anyone, so we lay down on the floor. But at four a.m., we had to leave again and walk on foot through the jungle. Two hours later, we reached a road and took a commercial truck and met up with some other people. The leader said, "To avoid the police, you have to take a shortcut to the coast. Follow this Cambodian man." Then she was gone.

The man walked in front of a group of people, fast enough to indicate how familiar he was with the area. He whacked at the undergrowth with a machete to make way for the rest of us, about thirty-five people. We'd walk for two hours, rest fifteen minutes, then walk again.

Suddenly I heard gunshots. Everyone dropped to the ground and the Cambodian leader vanished. Two Vietnamese soldiers carrying AK47's appeared. One of them said, "I'm a security guard in this forest. If any one of you wander too far in here, you'll get lost and die. I've worked here for three years, and I still get lost." Some people got up and ran back to the group; nobody said anything. He continued, "You have a chance for a better life. You can escape, but I'm poor. I don't have a chance. So I wish you luck, but I also need your help." The soldier was young and nice. Even now, I still remember him and what he said. Everyone looked at each other. Someone passed a straw hat around. I put my watch in it and my sister put in some Vietnamese money. We thanked him and gave him the hat as a gift. About ten minutes later, the Cambodian guide reappeared and when we arrived at the seashore about three hours later, I was astonished by how many people were there waiting for boats.

We left at eight p.m. Thirty-five of us in a motorboat that was big and new. The captain was Cambodian, and the boat moved smoothly across the water. I slept soundly from utter exhaustion. In the morning, the sun shining into the boat, I heard people shouting, "Land. Land. We see land. Thank God."

My sister and I were so happy. My two older sisters were still in Songkla and I was sure we'd meet up with them. I wouldn't have to stay too long in the camp, and my parents would be overjoyed to hear the good news. But then suddenly I saw a big ship and it was moving toward us. Thailand was written on the bow. It was a Thai naval ship and it made our boat look like a little toy. A Thai soldier stood out on the deck, threw us a rope and said loudly and in English, "Tie it. Refugee camp closed. Out. Go back Vietnam."

I translated for my boat and the people said, "Beg them to save us," because in the meantime, the Cambodian captain had jumped into the sea and, holding onto an empty twenty-gallon plastic jug, had swum back to land. No captain and no compass, so I begged them, but the soldier shot at the rope to break it which made our boat rock a little bit and then recover its stability. But when the soldier did the same to another boat, I watched as it capsized. We pulled two men aboard our boat, but the rest of the people drowned in front of my eyes.

For ten days, we drifted at sea with nothing to eat or drink. Sometimes it rained and we caught and drank the rainwater. Sometimes Thai fishermen jumped into the boat and stole everything they could, jackets, watches, necklaces and shoes. On the seventh day my boat landed on a desert island. The only living thing on it were monkeys, but the two men who climbed onto it from our boat found nothing else there but skulls.

I was dehydrated and starved. I couldn't even pray anymore. The people on my boat wailed and screamed. Then, on the tenth day, we were rescued by the Cambodian police, but by then I'd gone unconscious.

My sister and I recovered for three days in a small clinic on the Cambodia-Thailand border. When we were released, the Vietnamese soldiers there showed us the way back to Vietnam.

Once home, I stayed in the hospital for one month, suffering from migraine headaches, and because of such an extended absence, I lost my job at the middle school. Then in June of 1988, six months later, I tried again, taking the same route, but this time my sister, Huong, did not come. So I went by myself, and this time, on my eleventh attempt, I escaped.

Nghia Ngo

Born 1982

Translated by Hue Nguyen

I lived in the Sixth District of Ho Chi Minh City, which they're now again calling Saigon. My father made the plastic thread for fishing nets. My mother took care of my older brother, two older sisters and me. Before my younger brother was born, when I was two or three years old, my mother sent me away to live with a friend of hers. I don't really know why. I guess she didn't have time to take care of me. I don't remember being sad or missing my family and sometimes my parents came to visit me. I was also already familiar with my mother's friend who I called Sam, which is Mommy in Chinese.

Her house was two stories high. The top floor was one big room, where we slept, and a curtain divided the ground floor room into two rooms. Her house was triple the size of my family's. My mother's friend was about forty-five or fifty years old. She was married, and she had a daughter who was also married, but she didn't have any nephews or nieces. She was very kind to me.

In the morning, I woke up at seven o'clock and I ate a breakfast of milk, French bread and sometimes soup. My mother's friend also had some chickens, and I remember liking them and thinking they were funny. Sometimes I looked for their eggs and when I found them, I would run to give them to Sam. I also helped her chop wood for the stove. In the afternoon I ate a Vietnamese lunch of rice and chicken, and afterwards, in the afternoon, I would sleep for maybe two or three hours. In the evening, before dinner, I took a shower and when dinner was over, I turned on the television. I would watch until I was sleepy, and then I'd go to bed.

I returned to my own family when I was five or six. I missed living with Sam, and I cried a lot. I asked my father to bring me back and let me visit her. Even when I grew up, I visited her. She still lives in Ho Chi Minh City, and before I left for America, I went to her house to say goodbye and give her some candies. She congratulated me and told me she was happy for me.

Here in the U.S., I was working in the metal-finishing department of an airplane factory. I didn't like the job. I had to put something in the machine to clean a certain part and when I had to hold it in place, the machine would cut my fingers.

Then I got sick. I was sick when I was little too. It's very difficult for me to sleep, and I get headaches. I needed permission from my doctor to return to work, but my doctor would not give it to me. So now I'm not working, just living at home with my father, mother and younger brother. My older brother is going to college in Vietnam. One of my older sisters lives in Germany, and the other lives in Sweden. In Vietnam I sold automobile oil and air filters. Here, I'd take any job to help contribute to the family. But I will also continue to study English so that I'll be able to go to college.

Dan Tran

Born 1962

Translated by Hue Nguyen

I lived in the Seventh District in Saigon with my mother, father and nine brothers and sisters. I was only six years old, but I went around the neighborhoods and I knew everything. I knew the Communists were fighting with the South. I knew that some of the residents living in the city worked underground for Communist organizations and that they didn't kill civilians; they just killed the soldiers or the people who worked for the Democratic government. When we heard gunshots, my whole family would run inside and hide behind the sandbags that we'd piled into a big rectangle. The thick green plastic bags came from America, and we bought and filled them with yellow sand that was delivered by truck. I helped put the sand in the bags, and for me it was like a game.

On Vietnamese New Year's Eve 1968, there was a big battle. The American soldiers were fighting the guerrillas. The South Vietnamese army could not get into the city because the guerrillas had surrounded it. We stayed inside of the sandbags all night, and in the morning the shooting stopped and we heard on the radio that we all had to leave our houses and move into a church or a detention center. The Americans said it was for our protection and the protection of our homes. We brought only the things that were necessary because our mother had enough to do just to take care of the children. I didn't take anything. I was just scared.

It was early morning and about sixty degrees. Outside, it was very crowded. I saw some of the guerrillas standing in the street making people leave their houses and recognized some of them as my neighbors. They'd been working for the Communists, and now they wore the black clothes and carried AK47s.

We all held hands to avoid getting lost. Just a few people rode bicycles and motorcycles, but most people were walking. Everyone was scared, so everyone just walked quickly and didn't talk much. Our father went with us to the center and then went to the Catholic church where he worked as a teacher, to stay with the priests. The detention center had once been a big market, but now it was empty and the Americans provided us with food and supplies. Some people stayed in the center, and some went to stay with their relatives in the larger part of the city.

About a week later, my father told me he had seen the guerrillas shoot and kill three American soldiers. The other American soldiers were very angry. They couldn't figure out who the guerrillas were and who the civilians were; they only knew that a lot of people who lived in the Seventh District were working for the Communists, so they burned it down. The residents were not angry, though. It was a war, and this is what happened in a war. They didn't burn the churches and the schools.

After one week we came back to where our house had been. All the houses were just piles of rocks. The members of each family went to the churches to get sheets and cement from the U.S. government so that we could build tents. They gave us more building supplies than food, but my family had enough to eat because we had saved money and could buy it.

The neighbors got together, and we all helped each other build temporary houses. We used the stones from our other house and we quickly framed in the front. We lived in that house until we could build a more permanent one also made of stone and a corrugated iron roof. Then life returned to normal and I went back to school.

In 1975, after the Communists took over, school changed. The kids who had relatives in the Communist party were chosen to be the "nephews and nieces" of Ho Chi Minh and they were given red scarves to wear around their necks. They were the only students who got academic rewards. If you were Catholic, like me, you could not be one of the nephews or nieces of Ho Chi Minh. You did not get a red scarf to wear around your neck, and even if you were a good student, you did not get any rewards. They fired all our old teachers who had been soldiers for the South. The curriculum changed, too. In literature, certain writers were not taught anymore because they wrote too much about freedom: a poet named Du Nguyen, a short story writer named Khai Hung and a fiction writer named Nhat Linh. I didn't want to go to school anymore, but my parents made me.

I stopped when I was eighteen in 1979, because the government wanted to force me to join the Communist Army to fight in Cambodia. One night the police came to my house. They jumped over the fence and searched for me everywhere. Someone had warned my family that they were coming, so I was ready and hid outside, near the balcony. No one wanted to serve the Communist party, so all the men went into hiding and escaped. There were practically no young men in the country at that time. They had either escaped, were in the army, or were in re-education camps. So for women, it was very difficult to find a husband.

They didn't get me. They left, and the next morning they invited my father to the office. They said, "Why wasn't your son at home?"

My father said, "He's working far away."

They looked for me for a few more months, but I continued to hide in my house and they never caught me. A few months after that, I found a job as a worker at a government clothing factory and was trained there to be an electrician. Because of this, and because my brother was already in the army, the government gave me permission to work there for a year. Still, though, they continued to send me army registration papers. But then the company put my name on a list of "excellent workers." (You had to work day and night to be considered an "excellent worker.") Because my name was on the list, the government finally stopped trying to force me into the army. I worked at that factory for eleven years and I made fifty dollars a month. I felt frustrated, but I had to accept it because that was the way it was.

When I was twenty-nine, and had been working at the factory ten years, I met my wife. She also worked there. In 1990, the government began allowing people to start their own small businesses. So after one year, we married, and my wife and I quit our jobs. I bought a big sewing machine and made clothing that we sold and exported to Poland, Russia and other Communist countries. I hired another person to help me, too, and we made as much in one day as we'd made at the factory in a month. Still, all our business was in cash, and we had no contracts. If I sent one hundred shirts to a lady and she didn't want to pay me, I had no way to make her. A lot of people lost all their money and all their property. Sometimes it made people mentally ill. There were no courts for protection. I didn't feel safe and secure and I worried about my children.

Before we were married, my wife had had a U.S. sponsor, but we didn't really think about it, or think about leaving because it would take such a long time. We just worked and raised our three children. But then, after we'd run the business for ten years, my wife was called in for an interview with the U.S. Delegation. I went with her to ask if she could be sponsored now with her husband and children. Within six months the whole family got an interview and we were approved. I was so happy. The first thing I did was close down the business and stop working.

I left Vietnam in January 2000, three months after the interview. We had a party before we left with our neighbors and friends. I thought about going to a country with more civilization, a place that was much more comfortable than Vietnam. When I got here I was surprised that the streets were clean and paved. The transportation, the traffic was organized with traffic lights. The houses were built in an orderly way and surrounded by land. At first I didn't like the cold weather, but now I'm used to it.

Lan Ho

Born 1978

Translated by Hue Nguyen

I was ready to take the test to graduate from the twelfth grade in 1996, when I met my future husband, Tommy, at a party in Ho Chi Minh City, or Saigon. He'd lived in the U.S. since 1985 and was visiting his cousin who was a friend of mine. He didn't know a lot of the language, but he was more outgoing than Vietnamese people. Sometimes, when my friends and I joked and laughed about something, he couldn't understand us, but he didn't want us to call him by his American name. He preferred that we use his Vietnamese name, Nhan.

For the month he was there, we went out to restaurants and concerts together, and when he went back to America we had no plans to get married or anything. But he kept thinking about me, and after a year he got my phone number and he called me. We continued our relationship by writing to each other. At the end of 1998, he came back to Vietnam and visited for two months. He'd planned to stay only one month, but he didn't like his job and thought if he stayed another month, maybe he'd just get fired. But the boss told his brother-in-law, who was a manager at the company, to call Tommy and tell him to get back to work. After he returned to America, we just spoke on the phone twice a week and wrote to each other. Then, at the end of 2,000, his father called my father in Vietnam and talked about the possibility of us getting married.

My family was not happy about the relationship. We are middle-class and well-off. My family owns a small textile factory with four employees. There are also only three children in the family and so my parents didn't want me to leave. They were very worried. They knew if I stayed in Vietnam I wouldn't have to work very hard. I would just help in the family business. They also didn't know a lot about Tommy, where he came from, who his parents were. They didn't want me to leave, but I fell in love.

From what people said, I believed that if I came to America I could be more independent. In the Vietnamese culture, even when the children are very old, they stay with their parents. I'd still be living with my parents and they'd have to continue to worry about me. And even as a child I was willful and independent, and my father always thought I challenged the principles of my culture.

Finally, my parents just said, "Anything you want. You decide." So Tommy and I had a traditional wedding in Vietnam.

Tommy's boss said, "When you marry and your wife comes here I'm going to give her a job." So I already had a job waiting for me in Tommy's family's business. Two days after I arrived in America, my husband said I could go to work, but I didn't have a Social Security number yet, so I had to wait a month.

I was really happy to have a job. That way, I wouldn't have to depend on my husband for everything. And if I just stayed home, I'd just be lonely and wouldn't have the opportunity to learn anything. I wanted to get out and live life and learn about America. In the beginning, we put our money together in one bank account. And at first I couldn't do anything with it like sign checks or withdraw. My name was on the account and I had an ATM card, but I didn't know the PIN number. Now, though, I know what to do.

And now my husband and I quarrel a lot. He says to me, "I know everything, and you don't know anything." He makes me feel like I'm not smart enough to understand anything here. I wanted to drive so I could work somewhere else, but he said no, maybe in two years. You don't know enough English. You can't read the signs or understand the policemen. I want to go to college, but my husband doesn't want that either. I don't know why. He says, your English is still not good enough and if you go, you have to pay tuition. But I'll apply for financial aid. If I don't try, how will I know? I want to apply, even if I don't get in.

I want to discuss things, but my husband only wants to give me orders. I don't want a husband who controls his wife. I want a marriage in which I have some control too, a marriage of mutual respect. I don't know what the future will bring; I can't say. But in Vietnam it would be much more difficult to get out of a marriage. Here, I don't feel trapped. Here, I feel I have choices.

Sister Le-Hang Le

Born 1953

Written by Sister Le-Hang Le

I had graduated from the Buddhist Advanced Institute and had, with other Buddhist nuns, appealed the death sentences of two Buddhist monks, Thich Manh-That and Thich Tue-Si. Since then, the Communist police had followed me. I'd been forced to hide in different Buddhist houses, and I made several attempts to escape from Vietnam. They had all failed, though, so I planned to go back to live in the temple with my Dharma teacher and Dharma sisters. But while I was still living in a fellow Buddhist's apartment in Saigon, my friend, Sen, unexpectedly visited me. I knew her from Temple Long-An where I first entered to practice Dharma and had not seen her for five years. We were very happy to see each other, but whenever we went outside she acted scared and nervous. I asked her what was wrong.

She whispered, "Do you want to escape from the country again?"

I said "I can't. I have no money."

She said that if my brother in America promised to pay, she would ask the organizer to allow me to go.

"When would we leave?" I asked.

"Next week," she said.

I told her that I had no telephone and could not get an answer from my brother that quickly.

She said, "If you want to go, take two pairs of clothes and some money."

The next day, another friend, Van, came to visit me. After we said hello and talked a while, Sen called me into another room and told me that Van was the organizer. She told me to ask her to take me.

I hesitated. I felt embarrassed. I met Van every week, but she had never mentioned it to me. Then, after an hour of conversation, Sen was brave enough to ask.

Van looked at me, surprised, and said she thought I was planning to move back to Central Vietnam. Then she asked me if I could pay. I said, "My brother will be able to pay once I get to a refugee camp," and at her request, I gave her my brother's address.

I could not say a word to my roommates because the trip was illegal. On the morning of March 11, 1989, Van brought a ten-year-old girl, Tra, to my place and told me to leave immediately. She said, "Take care of this girl." My friends and Dharma sisters in the apartment did not know where I was really going. Fear, worry, hope and sadness mixed in my heart, and my mind was bewildered. I tried to concentrate and pray for the trip. I hired a tricycle to carry Tra and me to the bus station. Tra was a quick and talkative girl. She looked older than her age and seemed to feel comfortable with me. She told me that she knew her mother asked me to help her through the trip, and that she would listen to me. After I agreed to care for her, I considered her my niece.

While I waited to buy a ticket to go to Can-Tho, south of Saigon, I saw Sen and her daughter in another line. We looked at each other, but we did not greet or talk to each other. I got on the same bus with Sen, but she sat in the row in front of me. After five minutes, another friend of mine got on the bus, but we did not say anything. We sat like yogis in meditation. Suddenly, a shaggy looking woman got on the bus and said loudly, "People on this bus seem to always escape from the country." I was very frightened to hear that, and I tried to pray more enthusiastically. The woman tried to threaten other people on the bus, and she talked louder and louder until she finally got off and we left the station.

It took seven hours to get to Can Tho. By the time we arrived it was five p.m. I was like a pilot who had lost his compass. I did not know what to do and where to go. Luckily, Sen asked me to share a room with her in an inn which was located next to the market. The inn had two floors, and each floor had four bedrooms. On the ground floor was a common dining room and bathroom. Our bedroom just had one bed in it, no lamp, table, or chair. Sen let me sleep on the bed, and she, her daughter, and Tra slept on the floor. At the inn we also met a friend who'd traveled with us on the same bus, but still, we all had to treat each other like strangers.

Sen told me if someone asked me what I was doing in Can Tho, I had to say that I was visiting my friend's family to pay my respects to her father who just died last week. So, after we rented the room, we went out to have dinner, then stopped at the market and made sure someone saw me buy some flowers, fruits and two bundles of incense—things I would have given to someone in mourning. Sen also bought two half-gallon plastic cans for water and some roots of jicama to eat. Jicama quenches your thirst and makes you feel full. It was something a lot of people bought before they escaped which made the merchant suspicious enough to ask us if that's what we were planning to do too. But Sen coolly told her that we were vegetarians, so the cans were for soy sauce, and the roots were for soup.

Back at the inn we slept until 4:00 am. It was still dark, so I sat on the bed and prayed until dawn. While we ate breakfast in the dining room, a woman suddenly appeared, snapped her fingers, and left. Sen said, "Let's go."

Sen, her daughter Nhung, Tra and I followed the woman to the bank of the small river to wait with about thirty people for the boat. When the boat stopped, a crowd of people got on, and I heard one woman say, "Oh my God! These people plan to escape! Why else would the boat be so crowded today? I don't know any of these people. Who are they?" She was the only one speaking. The rest of us kept silent until we all disembarked on the opposite bank.

Our leader told us to wait for her in the open market along the river. Sen led her daughter and Tra into the market, and asked me to wait for the leader under the big tree. I stood there for many long hours. Finally, I sat on the root of the tree to rest my legs. A Chinese-Vietnamese woman whose shop was behind the tree had noticed me, and she invited me inside to sit. I told her that I was waiting for my friend in the next village to come to pick me up. "If I sit inside the shop," I said, "my friend will not see me."

She asked me what I was planning to do at my friend's house, and where the village was. I told her that I was going to pay my respects to my friend's father who died last week in Chuong-Thien. She said, "That's not very far from here," and suddenly, she called her son to give me a lift there by a bicycle. All I could do was thank her, then quickly leave the tree and walk up and down the market until I saw Sen. I told her what happened and Sen was upset. She asked me to buy something even if I didn't need it, and make sure people saw me putting it in the bag.

When the market was about to close, and when people were going to go home, the leader gestured for us to follow her. She led us to a floating dock, and I saw a small boat there waiting for us. Twelve people got into the boat. Not one person said "hello" or asked a question. The boat carried us along the river until it was midnight; then it parked under a thick bush to wait for another boat.

Hope existed in my heart, and it encouraged me to keep going. I continued to pray for everyone on the trip to be safe, but the sounds of dogs barking and infants crying from the village echoing across the river,made me feel very sad. I really missed the temple and my friends. The scene was very still, the people in the boat so quiet that it seemed everyone had stopped breathing. Even the children did not make a noise because their parents had given them sleeping pills. We probably waited there for only a half hour, but it felt like the whole night.

Then I saw a flashlight in the distance blink on and then off. I trembled in fear of the border guards. The leader in the boat said softly that if that was the border guards' light, we would have no way to escape. When the big boat approached us, the pilot made another sign with the flashlight that the leader in our boat recognized. The boat that approached was forty-nine feet long and twelve feet wide. It was made of wood and it was usually used to carry goods along the big river. The pilot and some other men reached down and pulled the women and children in our boat up into theirs. The wall of the boat was high and there was no step off of it so I fell from the top of the rail right onto another woman. She yelled at me, then quickly apologized for making noise.

It took a day and a half for the boat to carry us from the river to the territorial waters. And the boat had to stop twice more to pick up other people before it traveled directly out into the Pacific Ocean. On the first day, the boat moved steadily and smoothly, and I imagined that Boddhisattva Quan Am supported and protected all the people and me. However, on the second day there was a big explosion, and I heard the sound of the engine grow weaker and weaker until it completely stopped. Different thoughts came to my mind. I thought the Buddha did not protect me at all. Maybe the people and I collectively shared bad Karma.

The pilot, mechanic and some men in the boat tried to fix the engine, but it did not work. We drifted at sea for two days, but because the boat was out of Vietnam's territory, the Vietnamese Communist Coast Defense could not arrest us.

It was March, so the sea was calm, and the boat did not rock too much. After two days, though, I was very tired. I put the plastic can of water under my head and slept soundly. When I woke up, I was thirsty but when I reached for my water, it wasn't there and I realized that someone had stolen it. Sen gave me one cup of her water. How kind she was to me!

Death and life are like turning your hand up and then down. While they tried to fix the boat, the people asked me to light incense and pray, so I crawled up to the head of the boat, lit the incense, and sincerely prayed. However, the engine still did not work. Some old women cried, and some middle-aged women prayed with me. Some other women helped the men to bail out the boat. On the third day, we saw a very big dark orange ship crossing the sea, and all the men and women in the boat waved their clothes and yelled, "Help! Help! Help!" Slowly the ship turned in our direction and the people in the boat celebrated. But when the ship was about two miles from us, the pilot must have looked at us through a telescope and thought that the men in our boat were pirates.

So when the ship crossed on our path, it sailed on. The waves from its wake flowed over our boat, and made us rock from side to side, each time taking on more water that we had to quickly bail. At that moment I thought of death. Women were crying. They asked me to pray for them. I told them that I could not pray alone for everyone; they had to pray with me. Everyone had to sincerely pray with me. After that, one woman who had cried a lot lit a whole bundle of incense and passed it around to each adult. On the third night, we all prayed together.

In the afternoon of the fourth day, two big Thai fishing boats spotted us. They must have seen women and children on the deck, because they sailed directly to us. But the Thai flags on their boats made the people on my boat scream and cry. They knew of how the Thai pirates killed men and raped women. I was not panicked enough to cry, but I was still nervous and tried to pray more fervently.

The people asked me to wear my yellow robe and climb up to the roof of the wheelroom so I'd be in full view of the Thai boats. Most Vietnamese thought that Thailand was Buddhist country, and if the Thai respected Buddhist monks and nuns, they would not harm us. Two men boosted me up. I had to cover my head with the yellow robe to protect myself from the hot sun. The two Thai fishing boats sailed near but they did not go directly to us.

Then the people in my boat were afraid of being left again, and they again cried out. However, the Thai only made a gentle circle around our boat so as not to swamp us with their waves. The women and children sat on the deck floor while the men hid below.

The Thai anchored their boats about one hundred feet from ours. Then they threw big ropes and drew our boat closer. First, they brought on our children and gave them milk, eggs and juice. Then came the women who they encouraged to bathe and eat, though I chose not to bathe in the Thai boats, but I did drink water and have some food.

Thai sailors tried to fix our engine the rest of that afternoon and through the night, but they were not successful. The Thai said that they had sailed into Vietnam's territorial waters to fish, but the Vietnamese Communist Coast Defense chased them out. It was on their way back to Thailand that they'd seen and rescued us. We all thanked them, and several men and women offered them gold and asked if they would take us to shore, but the Thai fishermen said that their government did not allow them to carry any boat people to land. If they did that, they would be handcuffed and jailed.

Several women and men knelt down in front of them to beg, but they shook their heads. Once I saw that, I wrote down March 15, 1989, and then my name and the names of Sen, her daughter, Nhung, Tra, some passengers and what had happened to us. Then I put the paper into an empty plastic can and tightly sealed the lid. If our lives were lost at sea I knew the plastic would float onto shore and one day, someone would pick up the can and know of our fate.

After another long day of working on the engine, still without success, the Thai sailors informed us that they had to return to shore. If they were late, they would lose their business. All the men, women and children knelt down in front of them to beg for their help, and finally it moved the Thai's hearts. The pilot said that they would tie the rope to our boat and tow us closer in.

After one day and one night, the Thai cut the rope and left us at sea. It was sunset, and the people in the boat were very hopeless. We did not see the shore, and still had no engine. The people asked me to pray and I asked them to pray with me. Some people joined me, and others just looked at me dully. While we were praying, the men were still working on the engine and suddenly we heard it start. Everyone cheered.

The pilot sailed the boat for one night and half the day, but then the engine broke again. It was in the afternoon, and some Thai fishing boats were still at sea. People in the boat were afraid of Thai pirates and asked me to wear my yellow robe again. Luckily, the fishermen were very kind again. One Thai fishing boat sailed toward us, and the Thai mechanic helped fix the engine. He gave us a new belt for it, and that made it work. The crew from the other boat threw us rice, eggs and boxes of juice. The Thai pilot also showed us a shortcut to land. Most of the people had wanted to go to Malaysia. They'd heard about the Thai's maltreatment of refugees. However, the engine was not good enough to go further, and the pilot did not know how to get to Malaysia anyway.

While the boat moved slowly in the sea, we saw two sea birds in the distance and so we knew that land was near. By that time, the people did not care whether we landed in Thailand or Malaysia, and several men and women bailed water out of the boat, so that we could go faster. After two hours of hard work, we saw the shore but we were still afraid of the Thai who often arrested the boat people and put them in jail, so we anchored about a half mile from the shore.

After a half hour of waiting, the villagers saw us and called the police. The police ordered us to move closer into the shore. Still, we had to anchor a hundred feet out because there was no dock. The men jumped into the water to carry in the children, old people and women. Those who could swim, swam, those who could not, like me, walked. Two women helped me to walk through the water, and I reached shore on March 18, 1989.

After an hour, the police divided us into two groups, one of men and one of women. Some families had children, and the children confused the police by running back and forth between their fathers and mothers. But after the children settled down, the police counted one hundred and eighty-three people. The police looked at the boat and at us and just shook their heads. I was afraid to look at the boat again. It looked so small and fragile. I could not imagine how it could have carried one hundred and eighty-three people over the Gulf of Thailand.

An hour later, the police ordered us to walk to the street where three police trucks waited to carry us to a Buddhist temple in Saiburi, Pattani, in the south of Thailand. The temple was located on five acres of land. It had a main hall or Buddha Hall, three large houses and four small houses. The head monk greeted us and allowed us to stay in the two large houses. The weather was very hot, about 105 degrees Fahrenheit. The temple had only one well that did not provide enough water for all of us to use every day. I often woke up early to bathe and wash my clothes. We stayed at the temple for a month before the Thai government transferred us to Banthad near the border of Cambodia and Thailand.

Banthad was the holding center for Vietnamese refugees who'd arrived in Thailand several years before. When I arrived there, more than two thousand Vietnamese refugees had already passed through there and had built the Buddhist temple, Catholic church, schools, clinics and markets. But Banthad was not a safe place for the officers of the United Nations, Red Cross, Thai government and other European volunteers who worked for the refugees, so the Thai government built another holding center for those who landed in Thailand after the March 13, 1989 deadline.

Because my boat landed after the deadline, I stayed in Banthad about three months, and then the Thai government moved us to the holding center near the Panat Nikhom transit center where we waited for political screening.

Life in the holding center was complicated and difficult. Even though we were not exactly treated like prisoners, we could not freely go outside. And the United Nations did not provide enough food for us. Men and women had adulterous relationships, and several young girls lost their virginity. Some women had illegal abortions and nearly died.

I was disturbed by what was happening in the camp and in order to make the time pass more quickly, I volunteered to teach ESL in the morning, and at night I conducted a group of Buddhists in chants and prayer. People in the holding center were allowed to contact their families in Vietnam and other countries, so I contacted my brother in Colorado. He supported me by sending me a hundred dollars every two months. I lived there, waiting to be screened, for half a year and finally was called in on Friday, December 13, 1989. People in my house pitied me because they thought that Friday the thirteenth was bad luck.

Two Thai soldiers escorted me to the office and I faced six people: an American legal consultant who worked for the United Nations High Commissioner for Refugees, the Vietnamese translator, two Thai officers, the secretary of the Thai officers and the interviewer. Even though every person at the table could interrogate me, only one person did the talking, asking me hundreds of questions from eight in the morning until five at night. The rest of the officers observed me and asked me some difficult questions at the end. The two Thai's faces were strict enough to intimidate anyone.

They asked me about my daily life from when I was born until my adulthood. Because I was a Buddhist nun, they asked me why I wanted to live in the temple.

"I am afraid of death," I said.

They all laughed at me and asked, "So you won't die if you're living in the temple?"

"When I was a little girl living through the war," I said, "I saw many people get wounded and many people die. I was afraid to ever live like that again, so I decided to live in the temple."

They went on to ask me lots of questions related to Buddhist temples, about some of the most venerable monks and nuns in Vietnam, and the reason I left the country.

The American opened a book and asked me about two monks who lived in An-Quang Temple in Saigon, Vietnam. He asked me where Venerable Tri-Quang lived and how he was. I answered him that Venerable Tri-Quang lived at An-Quang Temple and he was healthy. He asked me if Venerable Tri-Quang sat in a wheelchair.

"No," I answered him.

In the book he showed me a passage where it stated that Thich Tri-Quang was in a wheelchair.

I said, "The book is incorrect."

He asked me who was it, then, who used a wheelchair.

I said, "Venerable Thich Thien-Hoa. The most venerable Thien-Hoa was paralyzed because of a stroke five years ago, and the most venerable Tri-Quang was okay."

He looked at me, and his green eyes scared me.

At the end of the interview, the interviewer asked me to chant the Sutra that I chanted daily. I wanted to chant the Great Compassionate Mantra, but I could not. Since I had talked for the whole day without a glass of water, my throat was too dry. So I chanted the short version of Three Refugees to the Buddha, Dharma and Shangha.

When the four people at the table prepared to leave, the two Thai officers turned to me and asked, "Why were you here today?"

"Because I came to Thailand after the deadline."

They looked at each other, then looked at me and said, "Don't worry. Go back to the holding center and wait." But because they did not look particularly empathetic, their words did not reassure me.

The screening officers separated those who'd been screened from those who hadn't, so after I was screened, I moved to another house next to the holding center and it was more tranquil. After a month of waiting, I was called in front of the Thai officers. At first, I did not know what would happen to me and where I would go. The screening officers first selected women and children whose husbands and parents were already in America, and I found out that I was the only single adult in the first group to pass the screening.

Then I moved to Panat Nikhom, a transit center where everyone waited for interviews with the U.S., Canadian, Australian and European delegations. We called them the third countries. Vietnam was first, Thailand second and then came the third countries. Life in the transit center was more comfortable than the holding center, but it was still difficult to live in an unsafe environment. There was a Buddhist temple for monks and nuns, so I had one room there. I learned how to sew clothes and to knit sweaters, and I also learned Chinese, French and English. Every day I got up at four a.m. to chant Sutra Lang-Nghiem. One morning, when I came back to my room after chanting, I saw my clothes scattered on the floor. I checked my things and found that my watch had disappeared. Luckily, the one hundred dollars I had just received that afternoon was still in my book. The next morning, when I walked through the courtyard at four a.m., I met a Buddhist who often helped out at the temple. I asked him why he had come there early. He said that he worked for a restaurant at the camp market. I asked him to chant with me before going to work. He declined, saying he was late.

While I was chanting, I heard the monks scream, "Thief! Thief!" I began to tremble, and I could not concentrate on chanting, but still

I finished. When I returned to my room, glasses, dishes and plates in the dish rack were broken, and my books were scattered on the floor. I did not know who the thief was, but I believed that the only person it could have been had been very close to me. I never saw him again.

After five months of waiting in the transit center, I came to the office of the United Nations and asked the Thai officer, "How long do I have to wait to be interviewed?" She humiliated me by saying, "You are a nun, so you of all people should not be impatient." She made me very upset, and I cried a little, but otherwise, I just kept quiet. A month later, I was called to see the U.S. delegation. This time they asked me only one question: "Why do you want to go to the United States?" I said that I wanted to go there to study. And right then and there the interviewer said, "Disapproved." After that, I registered to go to Switzerland.

The next month, I heard my name on the loudspeaker telling me to report to the office. I was nervous, but I said to myself, "Why are you nervous? You haven't done anything wrong." I walked to the office and met some Vietnamese men and the American who had asked me tricky questions at my screening. The American interviewed the men and me, and then he passed out the applications for volunteer work. The next day, I had a job as a volunteer.

Every day, I walked to the screening unit to translate the appeals for Vietnamese refugees who'd failed the political screening. My boss was the same American who screened me. This time he was very kind. He told me how to do the job, he gave me dictionaries to use, and he gave me a monthly stipend. One day, when we were sitting around a table talking, I asked him, "James, why did you ask me such difficult questions? If I had not been a real nun, how would I answer you?" He said that thanks to his questions, I was accepted as a political refugee early.

While I was working with James, the Swiss delegation called me into my interview, but before I went, James called me to his office and asked me why I wanted to go to Switzerland. I answered him, "Because I failed the U.S. interview two months ago." James asked me if I still wanted to go to the U.S. but I did not answer him, so he said I could leave work to get to the interview. I still didn't respond. Then after taking fifteen minutes to calm my mind, I walked to his office again and said, "James, I want to cancel the Swiss interview." He looked at me and smiled.

The next month, the U.S. Delegation interviewed me again. While I was waiting in the waiting room outside the office, James walked in before me. He saw me, but acted like he didn't know me. Then he came out, and left the building without saying a word. This time, after only two questions, the U.S. representative said, "Approved."

Back at work, James and my coworkers congratulated me. And when I went into James' office to thank him, again, he did not say anything. He only smiled.

Time passed quickly. A month after the US delegation accepted me, my name was on the list to leave for America on January 31, 1991. I had been in the camps for twenty-three months before I was allowed to go the United States.

At twelve noon on January 31, 1991, the bus from Bangkok arrived at the camp to transport refugees emigrating to third countries. The bus carried ten of us. Some would go to Australia and Canada, and I was the only one going to the U.S. I looked out the windows at the countryside and it made me sad. I already missed my country.

I was startled by Bangkok, my first sight of such a large, new and beautiful city. The airplane took off at midnight to fly to Tokyo where I waited for the whole day to take off at six p.m. on February 1. It was a large trans-continental airplane and there were not many people on the flight, so I had two seats to myself. A businessman lifted the armrest between three seats, lay down and slept for the whole trip.

The flight attendants had closed all the shades so I could not see the sky, but after seven hours flying across the Pacific, the flight attendants opened them and I looked out. At first I did not see anything since the sky was still dim, but as the plane continued to fly east little by little the sky brightened. Then suddenly, it became very bright and I said, "Oh! America!"

A Name Like Me

For Sister Elana Killilea

and the Board of Directors

of the

Asian Center of Merrimack Valley Inc.,

with

gratitude for their service to the

Merrimack Valley's Asian community.

 Introduction

There is a poem called "Name Giveaway," written by a Nez Perce-Tsimshian Native American, and it goes like this:

> That teacher gave me a new name…again.
> She never even had feasts or a giveaway.
>
> Still, I do not know what "George" means;
> And now she calls me "Phillip."
>
> Two Swans Ascending From Still Waters
> Must be a name too hard to remember.

Perhaps I was being presumptuous, and I knew I was going on blind speculation, but I read this poem at the first meeting of the Asian Young Adult Writing Workshop because all but one of the eight students who sat before me had names that did not come close to sounding like Suzy, Joe, Harry or Jane. And since my mission was to encourage them to write about issues related to being Asians or Americans of Asian descent living in Lawrence, Massachusetts, I thought maybe names, their names, would be a place to start.

"So?" I said, shutting the book. "What do you think?"

Silence.

"Did you like it?"

One nod. A shrug.

And not bold enough to flat-out ask if they'd related to it, or if they'd ever had any experience similar to the poet's, I blabbered on about names and identity, Ellis Island immigrants and how my name sounds Irish, and is usually a nickname for Margaret, but how actually I'm not Irish and my name really isn't Margaret and… and …silence.

Then Phuong Thai spoke. She said that her high school friends had called her Ashley, Phoebe and sometimes they called her Fe Fe and she never really knew why. And then Viseth said that people called him Vincent and Seth, but he was pretty used to it. George said he didn't know his Vietnamese name or whether he had one, but that his middle name, which was definitely not American, was really cool. And Sida said she didn't like her name. And then no one said anything else. So, okay, I thought, might as well tell them to open their purple folders, take out their white legal pads, and see if they had any more to say about it in a poem.

They did. In poems and in essays, they had a lot to say about a lot—because Sister Elana, who was then the director of the Asian Center of Merrimack Valley Inc., was right. She believed that an Asian Young Adult Writing Workshop would provide the students who joined, companionship and catharsis. Here was their opportunity to clarify and untangle complex and often contradictory feelings and their chance to record and dramatize their profound experiences. Here, they were given the time and the support to finally and freely express themselves.

By the second class they had switched to computers and click click clicked away, plugged into music-blasting earphones and staring at their screens with concentration I could only interrupt by saying once, then again, and then again that it was time for a break. And then ten minutes later, they were at it again. Writing, revising, editing and more revising, occasionally daunted by the difficulty of meeting the demands of the two forms they worked in, frequently irritated by my meddlesome suggestions, but always persevering.

The workshop ended with the summer, and its members dispersed. But the unquestionable honesty and courage that resounds in every word of *A Name Like Me* will make it endure.

My Name

By Sida Doung

I think I'm a strong, nice, smart, and understanding person.
I want a name that is like me.
Mine isn't.
But when you say it in Khmer it doesn't sound so bad.

Seeds of Lotus: Cambodian and Vietnamese Voices in America

Typical American Typical Khmer

By Viseth San

I dress in T-shirts with sayings on them like "Tastes Like Chicken" and "Rock On," faded blue vintage knee-cut jeans and blue flip-flops. I listen to music by the All-American Rejects, New Found Glory, Dashboard Confessional and John Mayer. I enjoy skateboarding and snowboarding. I eat pizza, chips and candy and drink soda. I hang out at the beach, the mall and the movie theater. I live in a home with a pink porch, rusted metal fences, white siding and white metal doors.

But when I set foot within those doors, I take off my shoes. Then I immediately smell fish sauce. A small lemon tree stands beside the door as décor. Recycled jars of soy sauce, oyster sauce, vinegar, sugar, salt and MSG are lined up on the windowsill and are lit by the late afternoon sun. Laid out on the table is a whole fish, a bowl of rice, fish sauce and a salad of pickled cabbages, cucumbers and bean sprouts.

Then a voice calls out to me, "A Own." It comes from the living room. Then I hear it again, but this time it is louder, "A Own!" It is my Mother. "Bott!" I reply. She calls me to the living room. She is across the room with her back facing me. I stand beside her and watch her. She places a bowl of persimmon and a cup of rice onto the shrine, and beside them are framed pictures of my grandparents and Buddha.

My mother wants me to pray with her. We get down on our knees, light three incense sticks and face the pictures. I hold the sticks between my palms and wish my parents longevity and great health and ask for my success in school. I bow three times with my head almost touching the floor. Then it is my mother's turn. She wishes for the family to be safe and to enjoy great health. She speaks to my grandparents and then takes the three bowls. We rise together and stick the incense into the cup of rice and persimmon.

It is 5:00 p.m., and the house is empty. My kid brother is at school, my older brother is at work, and my Dad is taking an afternoon class to improve his English. My mother is in her room watching a Thai love movie. I am eating the dinner that my mother made and thinking of tomorrow's quiz on Transcendentalism.

The phone rings. Dave, my college advisor, is on the other end. He is compiling a list of students' names that are going to show up for Saturday SAT class and he signs me up. Then I walk to my room and turn on my computer. I log onto the Internet and check my e-mail. A new message appears on the screen. It is a notice from Mr. M., the advisor of the Greater Lawrence Education Collaborative, informing me of Wednesday's meeting and asking me to spread the notice to all GLEC members.

There is a knock at the door. 5:40 p.m. My dad and my brother are home. My brother runs off into his room.

"How was school?" asks my Dad.

I reply, "Fine as usual."

He then reminds me about Mom's appointment on Friday. I need to be there to translate. I tell him I won't forget, but he insists that I write it in my planner.

I slowly walk back to my room. A list of homework lies on my bed. I start with the easiest: twenty-five trig function problems, followed by three chapters of The Adventures of Huckleberry Finn, an essay about what Huck symbolizes in his society, a few problems in chemistry and physics, and I have to study for an Italian and an English quiz.

Halfway through finishing my homework, I take a break for some cold soybean drink. My parents change into their sarongs and head for bed. My kid brother finishes his homework, watches TV and heads for his room.

It's 11:25 p.m. and I am finally finished with my homework. I brush my teeth, wash my face and watch the "The Simpsons." By twelve o'clock, the lights are out and the house is silent.

It's been a typical day of responsibilities to others and myself, a day of two cultures that I embrace and that have shaped me into the confident, out-going young man that I am. A life I'm so used to, that when someone asks about my origin, or when my family says I'm becoming less like them, I'm surprised and feel judged. But, even so, I like my life. I'm so used to it, it is hard to think of it being any different. Neither typical American, nor typical Khmer, I know who I am and will always be true to myself.

Seeds of Lotus: Cambodian and Vietnamese Voices in America

Dragon

By George Nhan

Second Grade was when I wanted
to change my name to Steve Turnbell
but then I heard from someone that it was too expensive
to change and now the name sounds stupid.

My dad named me after the president George H.W. Bush.
I don't really like my name
knowing that other people tease me
and call me Curious George or George of the Jungle.

Then in seventh grade
I found out my Spanish name, which was Jorge.
I didn't like it
because it had the sound of the word "whore" in it.
I tried to ignore it
whenever somebody called me by that name.

My middle name is Dragon.

First Day

I have a lot of memories about my first day at school. It was very terrible and I will remember that day for the rest of my life.

Step by step, I walked around the outside of the school. It was a big place with many students there. They were talking with their friends. And they didn't care about anybody else. But some of them were staring at the new students like they were aliens from another galaxy. Why did I know this? Because I was one of the aliens. I didn't know how to make them stop staring and talking about me. I just remembered what my mother told me before I came to school: "Don't be angry. You have to know how to control your temper."

Then I tried hard to find my line. I held the paper that told me my class number and my new teacher's name, but I couldn't do anything, just look around and find some of the Vietnamese to help me. But I was losing all my hope because no one had come yet. Maybe they were still busy sleeping. The questions inside my mind added to the noise of everyone talking and I felt confused: "Why am I here? Hey guy, wanna go back home?"

I kept walking and looking around like an idiot. One boy asked me, "What are you Chino guy doing here, huh??? Chino guy, do you need help?" He came up to me and asked me a lot of questions, but then I didn't really know what he was talking about. I just could say "yes" or "no" after each question he asked me. I gave him my paper after he asked me for it. And I wished he could help me anyway. He looked at the paper a few seconds, then he said: "What's up, man? We got the same class. Follow me! I'll show you where you can line up." I just followed him with an empty mind.

My class was glad whenever they saw a new person join into the line. They were so friendly. They made conversations with people they

A Name Like Me   173

really didn't know, like me. Their faces looked very happy when they talked to me. They asked me: "Where are you from? How long have you been here? How old are you?" Then I answered them by saying: "My name is Anh, I just came here four or five months ago, and I don't know how to speak English well, but nice to meet you." Then I looked at the sky, and tried not to think of anything. Everything got so quiet; they had stopped talking like they were in the silent film I had watched on television. I just saw them moving their arms or they just stayed there, munching their mouths to talk to each other… blah blah blah… then I couldn't hear any more sound around me… just silence, silence and silence until the teacher came.

I saw a guy with a big hat on his head like a cowboy riding a horse into the steppes. He said: "Everybody, line up… hurry up, guys." Wow, this teacher had a loud voice and a funny face. That's what I thought about him at first. Then all the other teachers came and picked up their classes, but we still stayed there and looked around. One boy said: "Do you guys want to find some ghost who wants to be our teacher?" After he said this we laughed out loud, then we gave him a nickname, Funny Guy. Time passed; no one stayed outside with us. Then when we saw him come out of the door, we yelled like we would never have a chance to yell again. I heard Funny Guy say: "Oh God, I never saw a teacher who looked like a penguin before." What's penguin mean, I asked myself?

Then we went upstairs into our classroom. The first thought that came to my mind was this classroom was so big. It was bigger than the one I learned in in Vietnam. Maybe my old classroom was half the size of this room. First, I tried to find my new seat; I was surprised when I sat near an Asian boy. I thought he was Vietnamese but after I spoke to him, then I knew he was not like what I had thought. He was Cambodian. I counted how many Asians were there. One, two… I was the fifth. I was glad when I knew this. I hoped all of them were Vietnamese, except the guy I had already met. But in life you never know; three of them were Cambodian and one was Vietnamese. It was a girl. She told me that she didn't know how to speak Vietnamese, but maybe she could speak a little bit.

When I went to the next period class, I got lost. I just stayed on the balcony, looked around and believed somebody would help me because I didn't want to give up. That's when I looked at my schedule. It was a square with a lot of symbols in it from two thousand years ago. Then I told myself: "I have no idea what the heck this schedule is about. What am I going to do?" I was nearly crying because I felt like I was disabled. But God gave me a chance. I heard the sweet sound of someone calling me. My mind said: "Hey, Anh, God sent an angel to help you!" An angel with long hair, blue eyes and the kind of face that made me feel like I had already met her a hundred years ago. She felt so familiar, but I couldn't remember her. I looked at her face again, very carefully; I felt that she was like my mom. I think she almost knew it. I did not know anything in this school, and of course I needed her help. I told her that: " Miss, I don't … know how… to speak … English … we… well, please… can you help me?" I spoke with many stumbles, and I was so confused. She tried to find my class. She went to every single class and asked them for me if I was in it and I just stayed behind her until she found the right one. When I went into the class, nobody wanted to talk to me. They left me alone. Someone even made fun of me. I did not care about them. I just sat there and waited for the time I could go home.

Long Sleep

By Giang Nguyen

I went to my room
There was a small room
I sat down on the chair
And looked at my computer

I turned on my music
I heard the sounds
It looked like waves
I felt I swam under water

The time I went to my bed
It was free
I felt it looked like long sleep
Long sleep needed for the people

Better Life

By *Tu Huynh*

My life in Vietnam was simple but it made me happy. I lived in my grandparents' house while I was in my childhood. I have many happy and pleasant memories of my childhood.

My grandparents' house was lovely. French people built it a long time before I was born. Of course, my granddaddy bought it from French people. Houses over there were not big. Some of them did not even have glass windows, alarms, backyards or garages. Vietnam is a small country with a big population, so houses seem like they have to squeeze a little bit. But my grandparents' house was as big as a house in the United States. It had three big rooms, two bathrooms and one living room. In addition, there was a big space like a room without any door, where I would take naps or play with friends. There was a big front yard and a wide space for putting chairs to sit and relax every night.

From when I was born, I lived with Mommy, Daddy, Grandma and Granddad. Every time when I was bored, Grandma always consoled me and gave me a hope to be living happily. I heard a lot of stories that Grandma told me. Each story had its own special lesson. She had told me the American Cinderella, and the Vietnamese Cinderella, folk tales explaining how fruits were created, The Three Little Pigs, the Little Red Riding Hood and many other Vietnamese legends. I really loved the way Grandma told stories. Her voice went up and down depending on the sections of a story.

Every morning, I walked to the market with Granddad. In the market, they set tables right on the sides of two streets. On the left side, there were fruits like litchis, plums, guavas and mangoes. On another table, cakemakers sold all kinds of little cakes. Those cakes were like tiny birthday cakes. You could even hold that cake in the palm of your hand. They also set out a big board in front of the table that said, "We receive the orders and deliver right to your home." There was a river of people walking on the street, and of course it was noisy. There were loud arguing sounds of some women yelling about the selling and sounds from kids whining when they wanted their mommy to buy something for them. It was enough to give me a headache. It was so fun, though. Granddad bought toys for me every time we went there. He usually bought me a little cake, so that I could play a birthday game with my friends when I came home.

I had two good friends who lived across from my house. Their names were Ngoc and Thao. Thao was my age, and Ngoc was one year older. We had been best friends since we were just three and four years old. Sometimes, we got in fights. However, we forgot about the anger quickly and were best friends again. We played so many games, and we always got mad at each game. Now, every time I think about the fights between us, I laugh aloud to myself.

The year when I turned four years old took away my happiness and sweet life. Mommy and Daddy decided to move to a bigger city, so that they could get better jobs and live a better life and also because my aunts and cousins were there. No one had told me I was going to move to another city.

That day was as usual as every other day. I woke up early, walked to the market with Granddad to have breakfast, and he bought me a Mickey Mouse balloon to play with, with my friends. I came home happily holding my balloon, and I saw a Titan truck parked in front of my house. Mommy, Daddy and my older sister, Yen, were packing stuff like clothes on that Titan truck. I thought they were playing a fun game. I was so curious about that packing game. I ran over to Mommy and asked, "Mommy, may I play this game? It seems fun!" Mommy looked at me with sad eyes and said, "Honey, we're leaving." My mouth opened. I asked Daddy again, and he still said, "we're leaving," with a sad expression on his face. Tears started running and passed by my cheeks. I ran over into the house to Grandma, let go of the balloon and hugged her, crying. I held her hand as tightly as I could and made sure that no one could take me away from Grandma and Granddad.

However, I still had to leave. Mommy carried me in her arms to get me on that Titan truck. I whined and cried a lot. I even tried to jump out of Mommy's arms but I could not. Now I was in the Titan truck and its doors were closed. I looked out to send my grandparents a good-bye look. Mommy consoled me by promising that she would let me come to Granddad's house for the whole summer. My mood was not better.

My precious time was gone and would never come back again. As Mommy had promised, I could go to Granddad's house and stay for the whole summer. I did that for seven years until I left Vietnam. However, it could not satisfy me. I have always wanted to go back to the old life living with my grandparents. Among everyone but Daddy and Mommy, Granddad and Grandma were the people that I loved the most. After I left Vietnam and came here, Granddad missed my parents, Yen and me so much that he started getting weaker and ill. I have been worried so much about him. And if I could have a chance to travel everywhere in the world, of course I would go back to Vietnam and visit Granddad and Grandma.

Seeds of Lotus: Cambodian and Vietnamese Voices in America

The Basement

By Phuong Thai

Strong winds flap the metal roof
She shudders
and folds her arms around herself
The floor squeaks
She feels the wall
and her heart
Beating…
grips the rails
and slowly
descends,
smells mold
dust
A door
creaks,
sees sparks of silver
reflections
She can feel it now
Click!
She opens her eyes
and there it is!
Light.

Seeds of Lotus: Cambodian and Vietnamese Voices in America

Graduation

By Sida Doung

At 1:00 p.m. while we were still in school, the teachers had arranged for all the eighth graders and their homerooms to meet up in the gym. I was sitting in the last row since we were sitting in alphabetical order. The parents would be coming tonight. The room smelled like sweat since there had been a class there before. There was lots of noise because the students were anxious and scared. The Principal and the Vice-Principal walked up on stage. Mrs. Baranski cleared her throat. She said, "You all have to be very well behaved tonight." After Mrs. B gave us a little lecture, the teachers began calling the names for the medals. I felt warm and began sweating. I was hoping to get the medals for Overall Achievement in math and history.

Ms. Coco read off the names for history medals. "Michael Carerher, Nolis Espanol." Now I got even hotter because I was always behind Nolis. "Brittany Flynn." What! She skipped my name. But I hadn't given up yet, because I was still waiting for two more medals. Mrs. Angelarie came up on the stage now to announce the math medals. I waited silently while Mrs. A read the names. Hey, she skipped my name again! But I still had a little hope. "Now for Overall Achievement" said Mrs. B. I now had the fingers of both hands crossed "Nolis." My eyes filled with tears. She had skipped my name once again.

We went back to get ready to go home. I was silent. Out of the four Cambodian girls, I was the only one who didn't get a medal. That made me feel disappointed and dumb. But at the same time I was happy for my friends. I tried not to look so sad because I knew in my heart that I had tried hard this year, and I should be happy just for graduating.

But the other reason why I really wanted those medals was because I wanted my mother to be proud of me. I wanted her to know that I had really tried hard in class, and that I was a good student. She was heartbroken when my older brother and sister dropped out of school. As an Asian it makes your family look bad, and it makes your parents embarrassed. When I got home my mother looked at my neck. I told her that I didn't get any medals but she still gave me a smile. I knew my mother wasn't as disappointed in me as I was in myself. That made me feel a little better. Still, I felt bad because I knew that I had tried. I also knew for a fact that I was going to try my hardest in high school. I wanted to become a lawyer and would be the first child in my family to graduate from high school.

Beneath the green eighth-grade graduation gown that I wore was a Khmer royal blue dress. At 7:00 p.m. I was in the gym once again, sitting in the last row. I heard announced: "Mrs. Nesbitt's class, please come up." I stood up tall, walked up to the stage and waited to hear my name. "Rodney Correa. Joe Desharnes. Sida Doung." My heart was beating extra fast now. I got my certificate up on stage and sat back down. I listened to Mr. Flannigan say, "I declare you the class of 2003!" My eyes filled with tears, my throat got even tighter, and my whole body felt hot. I went outside.

There, I saw my mother and my little sister. In my mother's arms was a bouquet of purple flowers. In another four years I will see my mother again holding flowers for me.

A Nick Name

By Giang Nguyen

My friends gave me a new name
It was: "Jinga Ling"
From the song "Jingle Bells"
They couldn't say my name right
Sometimes my teacher called me Chan
Because she thought my name was like Jackie Chan
Only one day
She called me Gi
I don't know why
So I call her Ms. Ryder Evil

Seeds of Lotus: Cambodian and Vietnamese Voices in America

The Cold Spring

By Tu Huynh

The weather was so cold, even snowing in the spring. It seemed mean to me. In Vietnam, it was always hot. Here, I was not used to the cold, so that was why it was not familiar to me. My Auntie walked me to my bus stop. The wind was so strong that it almost blew my scarf off. The snow fell down, and the cold made my nose run. Many buses passed by but none of them was mine. My Auntie and I waited patiently, but it did not come. Now, I was late. I sadly walked home with Auntie, and she had to drive me to school.

While sitting in the front seat in the car, I saw a lot of white houses and white grass because of the snow. Soon, the school was right in front of me. I was so afraid. While walking from the parking lot to the front door of the school, my head was full of questions: Are people going to be mean to me? How would I learn in a classroom without knowing any English? Does anyone in there know how to speak my language and would he or she translate for me? All of the questions were dancing crazy in my head.

Auntie signed my name in the book and a teacher with curly hair and a pink shirt came to take me to my class. In the hallway, people were staring at me because I was late and because I was a new student.

When I opened the door of the classroom, I heard people talking. The desks were pushed around and someone was laughing loudly because it was the break time. But with my first step inside the classroom, everything got quiet. Everyone was staring at me like they had never seen a new Asian student before. I answered them with a friendly smile. A teacher with a red dress and white shoes looked at me gently and asked me some questions. I did not know what her name was. I felt like my face was turning a little green when she looked like she was going to ask me something. What if I answered wrong? People would stare at me with funny eyes and start laughing. Luckily, she was so kind that she asked me easy questions and I answered perfectly.

Then she told me to sit at the empty seat that was set next to the Vietnamese boy. His name was Son. He was short and thin and it did not seem like he was supposed to be in the sixth grade. Others around asked me a lot of questions and my eyes rolled around and I said, "I'm sorry! I don't speak good English." After they heard that, they changed their attitudes and from then on, they never talked to me again. I felt like I was going to cry. The teacher introduced me to others and blah blah blah...I did not understand any word of her language. The only words I could understand were my name and, "She doesn't speak English well, she's a new student in our class." That was it. Actually, I had memorized my English lesson by studying hard the night before, but I was too nervous to say it.

Then the math teacher started the math lesson. I was thinking, what am I going to do if I do not understand English? Again she went blah blah blah...and I just saw some numbers on the board and some fractions. I understood some math problems, though. While she was teaching up at the board, some students were passing notes. If students in Vietnam did that, they would get in big trouble. Usually they would be hit on their hands or have to write a hundred times: I will not pass notes in class again. However, in this school, the teacher was not mean like that; she just took the notes and recycled them.

After the class, my teacher came over to Son and asked him to translate things that she was talking about so far and to tell me what assignments we had to do. But Son just told me two or three sentences about all the things that had happened so far. He told me the teacher talked about some operations of fractions and to do problems five, six and seven on page twenty-five. That was all. It wasn't because he didn't speak Vietnamese well, it was just because he was shy and mean. That was what I thought. In every class, I had to sit with Son. And of course he would always sit at a table of all boys, and I was the only girl.

Time went by fast. My classes passed quickly, too. It was all boring because I didn't understand what the teachers were saying. Finally, the dismissal time came and I went home on the bus. The weather now was better, warmer, and there was no more snow. The bus stopped at the bus stop. I saw my dad waiting patiently for me to walk me home. I talked a lot about the school day with my dad. I told him how boring the classes were and about the teachers and the kids.

That night, I cried.

My Room

By Anh Nguyen

Just like a little cave

Nice, quiet, but so dark

I just sit on my bed when I come here

I make my mind

Clear and strong, like a mirror

When I am listening, singing to

The sound of music

Rock & Roll, Techno, or Rap.

Seeds of Lotus: Cambodian and Vietnamese Voices in America

Accepting

By Samol Bo
for Rathana

I sat on my bed talking to my boyfriend on the phone. I told him that I missed him. I wished that he was there with me. Then I heard a sound of deep breathing over the telephone line distracting me from the call. Then I heard a click outside my bedroom. Then I heard another click and a weird noise and then a click. Then my dad called me. "Mol, come out here!" I said my goodnight and goodbye to Rathana. I put down the phone, and my dad called me again. "Mol, come out here right now!"

I entered the living room where both of my parents were sitting on the couch watching TV. "What do you want?" I asked.

My dad's face was red and his eyes stared sharply at me. He asked, "Who were you talking to?"

I replied, "A friend."

He asked, "*Proh or s'ray.*"

I didn't know what to say. I just wondered if I should tell him the truth or lie to him. "*Proh*," I answered. My throat felt like a frog was in it.

Then he asked, "Do you like him?" Silence. My dad asked me again, "So do you?"

I didn't know what to say. I knew that I liked him, but what was going to happen to me if I said that to my father? I just put my face down and stared at my feet. Then he asked me, "Who are his parents?" My mother screamed that his parents were Buu and Min. It broke the devil stare that my dad was giving me. My dad asked my mom, "The fat one who wore glasses at the Cambodian New Year?"

"Yeah, the one who wore the khaki pants and checkered shirt," she replied.

He asked me, "Him, is that the one you like?"

"I don't know," I said.

Then my dad asked me, "Do you want me to live a long life?"

I told him, "Yes, I do!"

"Then why are you doing this to me?" he said, "Do you want to become like your sister? She is getting engaged, and we don't even know if she is going to finish high school!"

I heard the door slam. I knew it was my brother. He came in the room and asked what all the fuss was about.

"She is becoming like her sister," said my mom.

Then he asked me, "Why are you doing this?" and just left to go to his room. Then my parents sent me to my room.

I lay on my bed and asked myself this question: I am sixteen; why can't I have a boyfriend? They think he is going to corrupt me, interfere with my education. They think that I am going to drop out of school and get married to him at this young age. They think my sister and me are alike. They don't understand that we are two different people. They just assume that we are alike. At this age, sixteen, they think that in this country no one can have a boyfriend. They say you can, but only after high school, then you can. But what if you don't finish high school or if you drop out of high school? How can you have a boyfriend or girlfriend then?

I turned off the light, lay in my bed, covered myself with the heavy blue blanket and just wondered. In Cambodia a girl at my age or even younger gets married and her parents don't say anything. Both of my parents got married at a young age. My dad's first wife was fourteen. My mom got married at age sixteen to her first husband. I don't want to get married yet. I just want to have a boyfriend. In this country they don't limit your dating age. You could start dating in kindergarten and that would be acceptable. People have emotions and we can't hide them. As a teenager in a Cambodian family, it is hard to date someone or to have a real relationship with your boyfriend. I had to meet my boyfriend in secret or ask my cousin to come along. I didn't want to lie to my parents but in this case I had to.

Spending time with him makes me so happy. He is the one who knows me best right now. Every night when I think about him, it makes me go to sleep peacefully. When he kisses me it just feels like I am in heaven. When he hugs me when I am mad at him it makes the anger go away. I can't be mad at him for long because everything he does makes me laugh. When we dance together he says sweet words like, "Oun, you dance so lovely and freaky." He loves me and I love him. The relationship is important to me now.

Days passed, I hadn't talked to or seen Bong Kana. Finally I saw him at the Laundromat. He held my hand fearfully. He asked me, "What happened, Oun? Why haven't you called me in days?"

"My parents forbid me to see you! They told me to break up with you! Which I can't do because the only thing that makes me happy is you! I love you, Bong, and we will be together." He told me that I should break up with him and he will wait for me. When he told me that, it hurt inside because I had to lose someone I really loved. I told him that it would be a long wait.

"I will wait for you," he said.

I know if I fight harder, my parents will realize that the more they keep me from seeing him, the more I'll disobey them and find ways to see him, just to be with him, when normally I am very trustworthy and responsible.

In school I try to be one of the good students. When they assign homework, I try to do my best on each assignment. This year my grades weren't as good as they were in freshman year, but I didn't fail any classes. I still got As and Bs except for Spanish. I still got a D in Spanish class, but learning a new language is hard. Still, I try my best. I know some phrases like "te amo." Since I started school I never got a detention and I try to be early. I was late only a couple of times because the bus came late. When my dad was in the hospital in St. Elizabeth's, I tried to visit him every day and stayed with him until visiting hours were over. When my mom gets sick I am there to help her with the cleaning and the cooking. When my parents need me to translate for them, I do the best I can. I don't want to be their favorite, I just want their respect. And I want them to realize that I am Cambodian and American, but I need to do what other American teenagers do in this country too.

Perhaps someday my parents will understand.

Dinner

By Tu Huynh

You could imagine how it was
When I got home from school.
Fried pork, cooked rice,
I smelled good food,
From the kitchen
Mommy getting ready
For dinner
I put my first steps in my room,
And teddy bears look gently,
A blanket folded neatly
On my cozy bed
Foot-sounds seemed heavy,
Daddy home from work.
A delicious dinner
In a warm dining room
I've always said,
Home is best!

My Life in Vietnam

By Giang Nguyen

I was born in Vietnam. I lived in Can Tho City until I was sixteen years old. I have a lot of memories from when I was a young boy and I went to school. The first time I went to school I was in kindergarten. I could not see my mom and I missed her. Gradually I began to make some friends and talk more. In high school I studied very hard because I had to study twelve subjects for one year. They were math, English, chemistry, gym, literature, biology, geography, drawing, music, handicrafts, physics and history. Every day on my schedule I had five subjects. The school began at 7:45 a.m. and ended at 11:45 a.m. everyday. I went to school five days a week. After school I went home with my friends or out to eat some food before we went back home. On the weekend I went with my friends to visit Ninh Kieu Port. There were a lot of restaurants, fruit stores, hotels, and flower shops. It was a busy port because for many years the U.S. Navy used it for their free time.

In the evenings, twilight made the river become more than beautiful. The wind blew from the water's surface, and it made people who were sitting on the benches feel good. We had a festival on the New Year with my classes and my teachers. Before the New Year people cleaned up their houses and got everything ready. On the New Year I saw a beautiful dragon dance, and I went to my uncle and aunt's house. I only had to say, "happy New Year," and they gave me money because this is an ancient tradition in my country. We went rollerskating, fishing and swimming together every weekend. In the summer I usually went to the countryside because my father was born there.

The village was named Long An and was very beautiful. The air was clear and there were many fields. In the afternoon I always slept under the trees. It was very warm, and that helped me sleep easily. In the fields, the farmers worked very hard under the light of the sun and it was very hot, but they continued to work hard because they wanted to have a good harvest for themselves.

Sometimes I went sightseeing in my country. I went to Da Lat where there was a city on the top of a mountain. There, I visited Than Tho Lake and Love Valley. There was a lot to see. It was very beautiful. I boated on the lake and saw Kamly, the Damry Waterfall, Spring Gold or Spring Silver, Dinh Bao Dai, and the palace of the last Vietnamese King. I saw the King's crown which was made of real gold and very heavy. I saw the King's dining room and his bedroom, too. In Da Lat, there was a mountain that looked like a sleeping angel, and the mountains were covered with banana trees.

I visited Nha Trang where there were many islands and a long seashore. It was very hot there. The sunlight was more direct, and I saw foreigners with very red skin. The seawater was warm and so transparent I could see down to the sand. At night I walked on the seaside and I felt warm because the wind blew from the ocean and I could smell salt in the wind. I visited Monkey's Island. All of the animals there were monkeys. I took pictures of them and gave them some peanuts, bananas and sugarcane. I ate a lot of seafood and bought souvenirs.

I miss my country very much. I want go back to my country because that's where I was born and grew up and all my memories are from there.

Home Sweet Home or Not

I am sitting in the shotgun seat
on a hot summer afternoon.
Ten minutes until the sun takes its course over the horizon.
Driving home from a trip to the park.
The silver Honda Civic takes a corner turn
and passes my old home.

35 Collogues Street apartment 1.
The brown and white house
where I woke up on hot summer mornings
and smelled lavender.
I used to hate the smell of it, but I miss it.
In winter I smelled strong scent of pine
raging over the thick white snow.
Then a black color drives as I think
of my grandma's death.

The lavender tree is cut down.
The house is now baby blue and navy and the feeling
It is not mine.
It belongs to someone else
I know as the car drives away.

Seeds of Lotus: Cambodian and Vietnamese Voices in America

My Friend Nghiep

By George Nhan

I have known Nghiep for four years. I met him when I saw him sitting down on the stairs during recess in fifth grade on the first day of school. It was a nice day out with a small, crisp, cool breeze and a clear, blue sky with light clouds that made some shade. I walked up to him. I first said "Hi" to him and then he said "Hi." Then I asked him what his name was and he said, "Nghiep." It was a unique and unusual name when I first heard it. Then all went quiet for a few seconds. Then I said, "Do you have any Pokemon cards?" to make conversation, and Nghiep said, "Yes." "Do you want to trade?" I asked, and he said okay, but he did not have the cards with him now and he said that he'd bring them tomorrow. I asked if he had a "Pikachu" and he said yes and I asked if he would like to trade it and he said yes again. So the next day, I traded my Jinx Pokemon card for his Pikachu.

Over the next few days at recess we would hang around the tall oak tree and talk about ourselves. Sometimes we'd play hopscotch and tag but we mostly just talked about stuff like events in the school, such as plays and fundraisers. I learned a lot about him. I learned that around the middle of first grade he was enrolled in Saint Patrick School from another school, that he played the piano, that he had a lot of people in his family, and that he shared a room with his brother Hung Co. But now he had his own room. He has about eight people in his family and relatives living in Wisconsin and he and his family go and visit them every year in the summer or winter. His favorite fruit is the durian and his favorite color is orange, but his favorite flavor for popsicles, candy and drinks is red.

In sixth grade, I was hoping that we would be put in the same classroom, but it turned out that Nghiep was put into a different classroom. In the lunchroom we had assigned seating, so we sat apart, far from each other. At recess I usually went up to him and we would just talk. Sometimes Nghiep played kickball and at times I glanced to see what position he was in. Most of the time at recess I would just walk around and watch the other kids play four square, tag or kickball. I still saw Nghiep sometimes on the weekends when I would call to ask if I could come over and play. But in sixth grade, I was the only Asian in my classroom, and I felt isolated. It was the same for the next year too, in the seventh grade.

In the eighth grade, Nghiep and I were in the same class but were seated in different positions. Nghiep was seated near the window and I was in the middle of the third row in the second seat. Our friendship sort of stayed the same, but we communicated a bit more. At least I wasn't the only Asian in the classroom this time.

Next year Nghiep and I will be in high school. We were going to attend Central Catholic High School and be in some of the same classes, but then I found out that I will be attending Andover Public High. Our friendship will still continue and we will still see each other sometimes and other times we will talk on the phone. I will meet new people at Andover High and hope to make other friends throughout my four years in high school.

Hmm...

By Phuong Thai

"Hi, what's your name?"
a pink-headed
man
asked, walking
out from Dunkin' Donuts
with an empty cup.
Uh, Phuong, I said.
"Fong?"
No, PhUOng.
"Foong?" louder.
Hmm...

"I have a friend,
and her name is Poo,"
he said,
...
"but you
know what?
You don't
look
like a Foong to me."

Landscape

By Tu Huynh

In Vietnamese,

The first name goes with the middle name,

And becomes a good meaning.

My mom and dad named me Tu Cam.

My mom told me it means,

"A very beautiful landscape."

My First Day in the U.S.

By Giang Nguyen

The first day I came to America, I arrived at the airport in New York. The immigration officials who worked there said to my family: "We will make green cards for you." They took pictures of us and after that, I took the bus to the gate for my airplane. At the gate I did not go anywhere because I was scared. I thought, if I go somewhere I will lose my parents, and I could not ask anyone to find them for me. At the gate I sat on a chair and watched the movies on the TV or listened to someone near me speak English. But I could not understand what they said.

We arrived in Boston at 7:00 p.m. I saw the sun because the time in the US was different from the time in Vietnam. My uncles and my grandparents had waited for us a long time. In the car, I sat in the front seat and I could see everything in front of me. When I went on the highway I saw trees and many other cars. I did not see any bicycles or motorcycles. I noticed that in America a highway was much bigger than a highway in my country. Before I came here I saw America on TV, and I never thought I would come here. My uncle asked a question. "Do you know how many cities we passed?" I said, " I do not know. Maybe two or three?" He laughed and said, "No, you are wrong. More than five cities."

Then we entered Lawrence. I saw the Spanish markets and Vietnamese markets. I could not read the names of Spanish markets because I did not know Spanish. I only read the name of the Vietnamese markets: "Saigon Market" and "Tan Chau Market." In them, I could find whatever Vietnamese foods I needed. I saw the buildings, bus station, post office and Lawrence High School where I knew I would soon go to school. The library was next to the high school, and I learned I did not need to pay money for the books. At the library in my country, they'd say to me:

"If you want to borrow anything you will pay money for it."

Suddenly, the car stopped. The bottom had fallen out. Everyone got out of the car. I was very cold and hungry. My uncle called the tow truck. Finally, we went to the China Buffet and ate a big dinner. I still do not know if my first day in the U.S. was good or bad.

My Name

By Samol Bo

At birth I was given a name… Samol
It means oval.
It's unique.

At home my parents call me Mol,
The proper way to say it in Khmer.
At school my teachers call me Samol.
But my friends call me
Bow-an'-arrow, Snapple, and Daddy Long Legs.
My boyfriend calls me Oun Mol, Babe, and Honey.

When strangers or new teachers ask for my name,
I tell them that my name is Samol but I
prefer Sam.
I don't know why because I wasn't called Sam
when I was younger.
It was Mol not Samol.
Nowadays call me whatever.
But I always sign my name Samol
To honor my name at birth.

Seeds of Lotus: Cambodian and Vietnamese Voices in America

Two Countries

By Tu Huynh

From when I was born, I have lived in two countries, Vietnam and the United States of America. I lived in Vietnam for eleven years and came here when I was twelve, so I have lived here one year. That was when everything changed, the culture, my life and my future. My feelings also changed. It seemed like each country had its own ways, and they were not like each other.

In Vietnam, my house was not big. It only had two bedrooms, a living room and a bathroom. So did other houses! I think that other houses were a little bit bigger than my house. I guess mine was the smallest of all. The front yard's surface was cement. It could keep a motorbike on it. Every day, my dad gave me a lift to school on the back of the motorbike. My school was close to my house, but Daddy never stopped worrying about me walking from home to school and from school to home. On the way from home to school, I passed rows of houses and trees. All of the houses were made out of brick and painted with different kinds of colors. Motorbikes connected into rows like long snakes crawling on the street.

After five minutes sitting on Daddy's motorbike, my school appeared and disappeared alternately behind some trees. My school wasn't big like the school in the U.S. In addition, we had to pay a lot of money for public schools over there. Teachers there were so mean. If you came to school without memorizing the lessons from the day before or without bringing your homework, the teachers would give you two hits on your hands or more. I remember once I came to school and forgot my math notebook and a pencil to write with. Then the teacher hit my hands. My hands were red, and I was about to cry. I really didn't like the way the teachers taught students. They were so evil. The night before the test, I usually stayed in my room and tried as hard as I could to memorize all the words in the lesson so I could do the test perfectly. I always thought that if I didn't do the test well, I would embarrass my parents and would be ashamed in front of my class, so I studied really, really hard. That made me really tired. But every time I got perfect points on my tests, Mommy or Daddy usually gave me gifts or something I wanted.

The education system in the U.S.A. is great! Everything is so cool and more fun than in Vietnam. It makes me feel really interested and light because I don't have to memorize stuff anymore. There are a lot of fun things to do in school. We don't have to pay for public schools and even some of the summer programs pay for students to come to their schools. That would never happen in Vietnam. In the U.S.A. every time I get stuck on some projects or some problems, the teachers are always willing to help me and never hit me. I like the way teachers teach students here.

There were only two seasons in Vietnam, rainy and sunny. It was a little boring with only two seasons in a year. But I liked the hot better than the cold. In the U.S, there are four seasons, spring, summer, fall and winter. That was so interesting with four pretty seasons in a year, but only I don't like the winter. It makes me sick and cold.

As you know, everyone likes to come to the U.S.A. for a happy life. So did my family. Mommy and Daddy really wanted a better life, so we came to United States for it. I didn't want to leave Vietnam, because there were a lot of things that I missed and made me want to stay. I really missed my relatives in Vietnam and the country where I had lived for a long time. But now that I have lived here a year, I recognize that the United States is a perfect country. Now I'm feeling happier. In the United States, I know that I can step firmly on the way to my bright future.

Home

By Sida Doung

I only hear
The drops of water
Falling from the faucet
Warm light shines through
I smell strong ginger
From the stir fry
Out the window I see
My neighbor's children
playing.

Two in One

By Phuong Thai
For my mother

Laura, Susan and I sat in the school library on Monday morning, waiting for the first bell to ring. I listened as they talked about their weekend. Laura excitedly talked about the rock concert she went to. "You-all should have been there! Linkin' Park was awesome!" she said as she flicked her red hair. "I can't believe I couldn't get their autographs, though! I waited for two hours in line!" She took out a small notebook with scribbles on some pages inside and pointed at a blank page where the autographs should have been. Her fingernails sparkled. "Well," Susan said, "at least you got to see them! I had to spend my weekend with my parents." She rolled her green eyes and sarcastically sighed. "They made me see A Walk to Remember with them. And my mom actually cried! It was SOOO pathetic." Then Susan turned and asked me how my weekend went. I lied. "Oh, uh… I saw a movie too. Spider Man, Tobey Maguire was cute." Either that or I'd say the mall. But truth was, I didn't go anywhere over the weekends. I usually stayed home to baby-sit my little brother so my parents could work overtime.

I don't know why I lied. Listening to them talk, I didn't like their sarcasm, their attitudes and expressions as they were telling their stories. I told myself that I wasn't like them. I didn't share many interests with them. I didn't listen to the same music, I didn't feel miserable for myself because I didn't have a boyfriend, I didn't freak out when I couldn't go see a movie the first day it came out. I was just hanging around with them because it felt comforting to be in the presence of other teenagers, American teenagers, even if we didn't have a lot in common. Then again, what else was there to do? I was the only Vietnamese girl in the whole school.

And yet, when I got home from school, I acted like them. I remember once when my mother and I were watching the news, I found her looking at me in disbelief after I rolled my eyes at one point to a reporter's comment and said, "Yeah, right," sarcastically. After only four years in America, my mother must have seen how much I had changed.

I remember when she took a photograph off the wall that had been taken of me six or seven years before. She stared at it for a while and asked me sadly in Vietnamese, "Why can't you be like when you were this little?" I knew she meant a cheerful and obedient daughter. From what she had seen, my shoulders shrugging when she asked a question, my talking back and the sarcastic remarks I made, my mother was afraid that I was no longer the daughter she once knew. I had become somebody she barely recognized. My mother was worried. She couldn't help it, but still, she let me attend a school where I looked completely different from everyone else. Perhaps to take control of the situation, she delivered long-winded speeches on how important school was and reminded me of all that she had given up for me to be here so that I could have a good education and in turn, a successful life. She told me to take advantage of the opportunity that I had. And then she reminded me that I was different. I was not like them, the American girls I hung around with, that I shouldn't copy their behaviors. "They don't suit you," she said. My mother was trying to protect me from breaking away from her, breaking away from the customs I'd grown up with.

Many times, after listening to her speeches, confused and angry, I questioned whether or not my mother and I should have stayed in Vietnam and never moved here. Our relationship has been complicated ever since we came to America. I couldn't tell my mother things that Heather or Susan or Laura could tell their mothers. I could never tell her about a new guy I'd met, or ask her for advice when I found out that Heather had been smoking or about my anxiety when it came to college. Then again, drinking, smoking and dating were the issues from the American culture that my mother had been trying to protect me from. Instead, our discussions usually revolved around what was going on in the news or my college scholarships.

If we had stayed in Vietnam, maybe everything would have been different. If we were still in Vietnam now, we wouldn't have to deal with the new American culture. I would never have met the young Americans that I hang out with now. I wouldn't have changed so much. My mother and I would definitely be much closer and understand each other better. Yet, if we were back there still, I might be unable to get into a college. I would be dependent on her for virtually every aspect of my life. I would still be living with my mother now and for the next seven years or longer. I would never have gotten a job to at least partially support myself, like I have now. Essentially, I wouldn't have the freedom and independence that I have here in America. And, aren't these the things my mother really wanted for me by moving here? I now have more choices and possibilities to have a good education, to have a career of my choice and in turn, a rich and satisfying life.

Perhaps I may not act as a demure and obedient Asian woman, but I can still uphold the values and beliefs of my upbringing. Though I must be more like Americans, strong-headed, independent and self-sufficient, I don't have to value the superficial things and be materialistic. I can still see the greater depths of things. I have not changed completely. Both Asian and American culture have made me into who I am now and I would never give them up. I am merely integrating both cultures in my one persona in order to find my success and happiness in life, which I know are the two things that my mother truly has wanted for me from the beginning. And so one day, perhaps she will grow to fully accept who I am and the person I will become.

Seeds of Lotus: Cambodian and Vietnamese Voices in America

My Room

By Viseth San

Nike T-shirts hang from a chair
Tommy vintage blue jeans draped over my bed

Homer Simpson drinks beer
Spider-Man climbs a New York skyscraper

The Adventures of Tom Sawyer leans
on The Scarlet Letter
The Scarlet Letter pushes
on the Cambodian/English Dictionary

A talkative box called Sony in one corner
And beside it a computer named Compaq

Above the bed where wall meets ceiling
A small platform, red with gold trim

In the center, a marble figurine
His body draped in a yellow sarong

His lips are relaxed and slightly parted
His eyes are fixed on me

Hands palm to palm, right leg folded back
He observes, all knowing, all seeing, serene

About the Editor

Peggy Rambach is the author of Fighting Gravity, a novel based on her marriage to writer, Andre Dubus, and a collection of short stories entitled When the Animals Leave. She is the editor of Seeds of Lotus; Cambodian and Vietnamese Voices in America, also published by The Paper Journey Press. She was twice awarded the Massachusetts Cultural Council Individual Artist Grant in Fiction, was the recipient of the St. Botolph Foundation Grant in Literature, was a Fellow at the MacDowell and Yaddo Artist Colonies and named a 2005 Literacy Champion by the Massachusetts Literacy Foundation. Ms. Rambach, is a resident teaching/artist in healthcare with grant support from the Kenneth B. Schwartz Center as part of the Healing Arts; New Pathways to Health and Community project in collaboration with the Massachusetts Cultural Council and the Vermont Arts Exchange. She lives in Andover, Massachusetts.

About the Cover Artist

Rosalvo Leomeu Vidal is from Arraias, Tocantins Brazil. He is a journalist, lawyer, poet, and lecturer on Ramayana and global leadership. He has dedicated the last ten years to an apprenticeship in fine art inspired by dreams of Lord Ganesha, Saraswathi Devi and Lord Buddha. Lotus Flower is his favorite theme.

Printed in the United States
61406LVS00001B/1-99

9 780977 315666